全国职业技能英语系列教材

职场
综合英语
实训手册

第三册

总主编　童敬东
总顾问　陆松岩

主　编　陈立伟　石　莉
编　者　夏　萍　马琳玉
　　　　石晓依　徐　静
　　　　秦　佳　孙宏兴
　　　　蔡　颖
顾　问　张国翔

Vocational
Comprehensive
English-Training
Course

北京大学出版社
PEKING UNIVERSITY PRESS

图书在版编目(CIP)数据

职场综合英语实训手册.第三册/陈立伟,石莉主编.—北京:北京大学出版社,2018.5
ISBN 978-7-301-29263-1

(全国职业技能英语系列教材)

Ⅰ.①职… Ⅱ.①陈…②石… Ⅲ.①英语—高等职业教育—习题集 Ⅳ.① H319.6

中国版本图书馆 CIP 数据核字 (2018) 第 033803 号

书 名	职场综合英语实训手册(第三册)
	ZHICHANG ZONGHE YINGYU SHIXUN SHOUCE
著作责任者	陈立伟 石 莉 主编
责任编辑	黄瑞明
标准书号	ISBN 978-7-301-29263-1
出版发行	北京大学出版社
地 址	北京市海淀区成府路 205 号 100871
网 址	http://www.pup.cn 新浪微博:@北京大学出版社
电子信箱	zbing@ pup. pku. edu. cn
电 话	邮购部 62752015 发行部 62750672 编辑部 62754382
印刷者	三河市博文印刷有限公司
经销者	新华书店
	787 毫米 ×1092 毫米 16 开本 8.5 印张 280 千字
	2018 年 5 月第 1 版 2018 年 5 月第 1 次印刷
定 价	35.00 元

未经许可,不得以任何方式复制或抄袭本书之部分或全部内容。
版权所有,侵权必究
举报电话:010-62752024 电子信箱:fd@pup.pku.edu.cn
图书如有印装质量问题,请与出版部联系,电话:010-62756370

前　言

《职场综合英语教程》是高职院校学生使用的教材，全书共三册。《职场综合英语实训手册》(第三册)作为主教材的配套，旨在融技能竞赛大纲和新人才培养方案于辅助教材中，面向全体学生，综合提升学生英语听、说、读、写、译的语言技能、职业素养和职业能力。

全书共分六个单元，即：Business Trip，Hotel，Shopping，Banking，Enterprise，Automobile。每个单元紧扣《职场综合英语教程3》主教材的话题，再结合历年的各类高职院校英语技能赛事，将听说读写技能训练贯穿全书，在设计各项任务时，依据由易到难，由点到线，由线到面，环环相扣，层层递进原则，一步步引导学生完成各项任务，降低技能训练难度，既遵循学习者的认知规律，又为增强学生听说读写能力提供了训练机会，大大增强学习者学习积极性，鼓励他们勇于开口，勇于参加各类比赛，努力提高学习者的英语技能水平。

本训练手册包括 SPEAKING 和 WRITING 两大部分（以第一单元为例）。

SPEAKING 为口语训练题型，分为 Section A 和 Section B 两个训练项目。Section A 主要参考高等职业院校技能大赛英语口语赛项中的 Presentation 项目进行口语训练，而 Section B 主要结合口语赛项中 Interview 部分进行项目训练。

Section A 设计成 Task 1 词汇练习、Task 2 句型练习、Task 3 段落练习和 Task 4 复述段落。

内容安排：参照高等职业院校技能大赛英语口语赛 Presentation 的形式做一个简短的导游词，共分为四个任务。在 Task 1 部分提供一些与旅行相关的单词和词组，让学生做配对练习，初步熟悉相关词汇。完成 Task 1 后，Task 2 是听五个句子，学生可以参考 Task 1 中的词汇，将句中所缺单词补充完整。Task 3 是听一段短文，让学生依据 Task 2 中的五个句子，补充完成 Task 3 的导游词。最后在 Task 4 让学生在完成前三个任务的基础上，再一次听这段短文，听后复述导游词，限时 2 分钟。

设计目的：该部分各任务间相互联系、相互影响，由单词到句型，由句型到段落，由点到线，由线到面，由易到难，环环相扣，层层递进，一步步引导学生完成各项任务，既符合学习者认知规律，降低技能训练的难度，又能增强学生的听说能力，提高学生的参赛水平。

Section B 设计成 Task 1 问答练习、Task 2 面试练习。

内容安排：结合高等职业院校技能大赛英语口语赛项中 Interview 的形式分成两个训练环节，逐步引导学生完成面试活动。在 Task 1 环节中，先让学生围绕一份与旅游有关的简历和搭档做问答练习，熟悉如何在面试过程中根据简历进行提问和回答，为 Task 2 做好铺垫。在 Task 2 环节中，设定学生身份，让学生分别扮演面试官和求职者，根据之前的简历内容做面试任务（之前完成的问答环节在这里就能很好地辅助学生完成任务）。为降低难度，这个环节给出了对话样本，学生可以参考该样本完成面试任务，也可以自己提取信息重新整合对话，相对比较灵活。

设计目的：这部分提供一份简历和相关提示问题，设置面试情景和面试角色，让学生做问答练习和面试练习，旨在让他们通过练习，掌握面试中如何组织问题、回答问题，如何开展面试对话，引导学生有针对性地组织对话，帮助他们顺利完成训练任务，提高学生参赛能力。

WRITING 为写作训练题型，根据主教材本单元的课题，结合高职高专英语写作大赛的要求和比赛形式，分为 Task 1，Task 2 和 Task 3 三个环节，提供范例，主要解决与图表相关的写作问题，旨在提高学生的写作能力和参赛水平。

该部分设计成 Task 1 学习句型、Task 2 学习组织框架、Task 3 学习图表写作。

Task 1　参照高职高专英语写作大赛关于图表描述的内容和形式，结合主教材本单元旅行的话题，让学生听五个带有画线部分的句子，这些句子既与本单元课题相关联，又能帮助学生解决描述图表时句型匮乏的问题。通过练习，让学生初步掌握图表写作题中所需句型，为之后的写作任务做好铺垫。

Task 2　该部分在完成 Task 1 的基础上，向学生提供写作框架练习，包括开头、正文和结尾部分。设计练习时打乱写作框架的顺序，让学生判断开头、正文和结尾部分，这样，学生对于如何描述图片、如何表示图片中的差异、如何组织这类文章就能有很好的了解。通过练习，一方面较好地降低了难度，另一方面也给学生的写作提供了方向，为下面的写作任务做好了铺垫。

Task 3　该部分结合当今旅游热点话题，模拟高职高专英语写作大赛的比赛形式，设计了一个与主教材本单元课题相关的情景题。学生可以参考 Task 1 中的句型练习和 Task 2 中的框架练习，从所给图表中提取相应信息，完成一篇有关学生暑假

前言

去哪里旅游的写作。

为了降低难度,让学生先从句型学习入手,再学习写作框架,最后提供写作范例。

《职场综合英语实训手册》(第三册)由陈立伟、石莉主编,江苏昆山开放大学英语教学团队中的夏萍、马琳玉、石晓依、徐静、秦佳、孙宏兴和蔡颖参加编写(排名不分先后)。在编写过程中,编写团队除得到编者所在单位校领导的鼎力支持外,还得到了北京大学出版社外语编辑部郝妮娜和黄瑞明编辑的悉心指导,在此谨向她们表示衷心的感谢!

在编写过程中,我们参考了大量的国内外参考资料,对这些资料的作者我们深表感谢。同时,我们诚恳希望各位教师和同学在使用本书的过程中把我们编写之错漏记下来反馈给我们,以便我们以后及时修订,使本书更臻于完善。

编者
2017 年 06 月

目 录

Unit 1 Business Trip ·· (1)
    Part Ⅰ   Speaking ·· (1)
    Part Ⅱ   Writing ·· (4)

Unit 2 Hotel ··· (8)
    Part Ⅰ   Speaking ·· (8)
    Part Ⅱ   Writing ·· (11)

Unit 3 Shopping ·· (14)
    Part Ⅰ   Speaking ·· (14)
    Part Ⅱ   Writing ·· (17)

Unit 4 Banking ·· (21)
    Part Ⅰ   Speaking ·· (21)
    Part Ⅱ   Writing ·· (24)

Unit 5 Enterprise ·· (28)
    Part Ⅰ   Speaking ·· (28)
    Part Ⅱ   Writing ·· (31)

Unit 6 Automobile ·· (34)
    Part Ⅰ   Speaking ·· (34)
    Part Ⅱ   Writing ·· (37)

Appendix   Tests
    Test 1 ·· (41)
    Test 2 ·· (54)
    Test 3 ·· (66)
    Test 4 ·· (79)

参考答案及听力原文 ·· (92)

Unit 1 Business Trip

Part Ⅰ　Speaking

Section A
Task 1

Directions: *Please match the following English words and phrases with their Chinese meanings.*

_____	1. on behalf of	a.	游客
_____	2. colleague	b.	真诚地
_____	3. local guide	c.	奢侈的,奢华的
_____	4. experience	d.	地导
_____	5. landscape	e.	风景名胜区
_____	6. sincerely	f.	代表
_____	7. luxurious	g.	风景,景观
_____	8. scenic spot	h.	经历
_____	9. downtown	i.	市中心
_____	10. tourist	j.	同事

Task 2

Directions: *Listen to the following sentences and fill in the blanks by using the words you hear. The words or phrases in Task 1 are for your reference.*

1. I _____ hope you will enjoy your stay in our city.
2. I'll do everything possible to make your visit a pleasant _____.
3. You're going to stay at the May Flower, a _____ five-star hotel.
4. You can easily visit the scenic spots and enjoy the natural and cultural _____ around us.
5. _____ the company and my colleagues, I'd like to extend a warm welcome to all of you.

Task 3

Directions: *Listen to the following passage and use the sentence patterns given in Task 2 to fill in the blanks.*

Good morning, everyone! I'm Lisa and I'm from Shanghai Youth Travel Service Company. 1 . During your stay in our city, I will be your local guide. 2 . If you have any problems or requests, please don't hesitate to let me know. 3 . Although the hotel is not exactly in downtown, it is strategically located with easy access to many tourist attractions. 4 . As you'll be staying in our city for five days, please do remember the number of our bus. 5 .

Task 4

Directions: *Listen again to the short speech in the "Reference Passage" and repeat or retell it in your own words. You'll have 2 minutes for preparation.*

Section B

Task 1

Directions: *Read the following resume and answer the questions based on the given information. Act out an Interview with your partner, the questions below can be used as guidelines. Now you'll see a resume.*

Unit 1 Business Trip

Resume

Name: Li Lu   Sex: Female

Birthdates: October 12, 1990   Height: 163 cm

Marital status: married

Career Objective: to work as a tour guide with Suzhou International Travel Agency.

Work experience:

* 2016—present

serve as a guide for foreigners at folk custom and culture village in Shenzhen, responsible for explaining China's various folk customs and cultures to foreign visitors.

* 2014—2016

worked as a guide for Hangzhou International Travel Service. Responsibilities included arranging, coordinating tourist activities, and offering service of transportation, accommodations, sightseeing, shopping and entertainment.

Educational background:

2010—2014   majored in tourism at Shanghai Institute of Foreign Languages.

Foreign language: fluent English

Technical qualification: received a tourist guide qualification certificate

Questions:

1. What's the applicant's name?
2. Is the applicant single or married?
3. Where did the applicant graduate and what's her major?
4. What career objective does the applicant have?
5. What did the applicant do during the year 2014—2016?
6. What technical qualification did the applicant receive?

Task 2

Directions: *Suppose you are Li Lu, the job applicant in Task 1. Your partner will be the interviewer. Role-play the interview with your partner. The following sample dialogue will help you finish the task. You can also make your own dialogue according to the given information in the resume.*

Sample Dialogue:

A: Good morning!

B: Good morning! What's your name, please?

A: My name is Li Lu.

B: Are you single or married?

A: I'm married, sir.

B: Where did you graduate and what's your major?

A: I graduated from Shanghai Institute of Foreign Languages and I majored in Tourism.

B: What career objective do you have?

A: I want to work as a guide for your company.

B: What did you do during the year 2014—2016?

A: I worked as a guide for Hangzhou International Travel Service. My responsibilities included arranging, coordinating tourist activities, and offering service of transportation, accommodations, sightseeing, shopping and entertainment.

B: Have you got the tourist guide qualification certificate?

A: Yes, sir.

B: And how much do you want to be paid?

A: 100,000 RMB per year, I hope.

B: OK, we finished today. Thank you, Miss Li!

A: Thanks for your interview! Hope to receive your good news! Goodbye, sir!

B: Goodbye!

Part Ⅱ Writing

Task 1

Directions: *Listen to the following useful sentences which can be used to describe the pictures and charts.*

1. <u>It is reported that</u> in recent years several new holiday habits have been developed.

Unit 1 Business Trip

2. <u>Based on the report we can see that</u> in 1998, 41 percent of people stayed at home to enjoy their holidays.

3. But now <u>the proportion has reduced to</u> 10 percent.

4. <u>The proportion of</u> camping and traveling abroad <u>was increasing steadily</u>.

5. <u>In short</u>, nowadays, people's living standard <u>has been rising greatly</u>.

Task 2

Directions: *Decide which paragraph should be the beginning, the body and the ending.*

Paragraph one:

Why did those changes appear? I think there are several reasons. First, ... Second, ... In short, ...

Paragraph two:

Based on the report we can see that in the year XXXX, XX percent of people... But now the proportion has reduced to XX percent. More people... The proportion of ... was increasing steadily, from XX percent in the year XXXX to XX percent in the year XXXX, and XX percent in XXXX to XX percent in XXXX respectively. On one hand,... On the other hand... In the year XXXX, XX percent people ... while in XXXX only XX percent prefer to ... What great changes!

Paragraph three:

In the modern society, more and more people like to... It is reported that... Among them, the most interesting one is...

Beginning: _____

Body: _____

Ending: _____

Task 3

Directions: *In this section, you are required to write an essay within 30 minutes based on the given situation. The essay should be more than 150 words.*

Situation 1

You are the secretary from May Tourism Company and responsible for *arranging travelling lines. One day, you received the PPT made by your partner as follows. Read the data which shows the changes in the way people spend their holidays. The table divides the tourism business into four parts, telling the different percentages in 1998 and in 2015, from which you will notice the trend of current tourism business and are required to write a report.*

WHERE PEOPLE ENJOY THEIR HOLIDAYS		
Year	1998	2015
Staying at home	41%	10%
Going to seaside	38%	32%
Camping	9%	35%
Travelling abroad	12%	23%
Total	100%	100%

Reference Writing: (*Read the following sample and pay more attention to the underlined parts in the passage which are helpful for your writing task.*)

Beginning:

<u>In the modern society more and more people like to</u> go on holidays in different ways. <u>It is reported that</u> the number of the people who went on holidays from 1998 to 2015 changed greatly. Among them, the most interesting one is that plenty of people prefer to go camping, rather than stay at home.

Body:

<u>Based on the report, we can see that</u> in the year 1998, 41% of people chose to stay at home and 38% went to seaside. At the same time, more people were interested in going camping, and spending their holidays abroad, from 9% in the year 1998 to 35% in the year 2015. <u>It has increased by</u> about 4 times. As for travelling abroad, 12% in the year 1998 <u>rose</u> to 23% in the year 2015 <u>respectively</u>. The number is two times as much as that in 1998. On one hand, <u>the percentage of</u> staying at home and going to see side <u>decreased by degrees</u>; on the other hand, the percentage of going camping and traveling abroad <u>rose dramatically</u>. What great changes!

Ending:

Why did those changes appear? I think there are several reasons. First, nowadays many people have plenty of time and money which enable them to go out to enjoy the beautiful scenery and fresh air. Second, with the development of society and economy, the consumers not only pay attention to the satisfaction of material needs, but also pursue the spiritual needs. In short, we intend to focus on our physical and mental health in order to relax ourselves after work.

Situation 2: *You are the secretary from May Tourism Company and responsible for arranging travelling lines. One day, you received the PPT made by your partner as follows. Read the data which shows the changes in the way middle school students spend their summer vacations. The table divides the tourism business into four parts, telling the different percentages in 1999 and in 2016, from which you will notice the trend of current tourism business and are required to write a report.*

WHERE MIDDLE SCHOOL STUDENTS ENJOY THEIR SUMMER VACATIONS		
Year	1999	2016
Staying at home	45%	11%
Going to seaside	35%	38%
Camping	7%	29%
Travelling abroad	13%	22%
Total	100%	100%

Unit 2 Hotel

Part Ⅰ Speaking

Section A

Task 1

Directions: *Please match the following English words and phrases with their Chinese meanings.*

_____ 1. global   a. 每年
_____ 2. range from   b. 全球的
_____ 3. luxury   c. 度假胜地
_____ 4. guests room   d. 愿景
_____ 5. per year   e. 奢侈,奢华
_____ 6. digital   f. 从……到……范围
_____ 7. flexible   g. 客房
_____ 8. be committed to   h. 致力于……
_____ 9. vision   i. 数字的
_____ 10. resort   j. 灵活的

Task 2

Directions: *Listen to the following sentences and fill in the blanks by using the*

Unit 2 Hotel

words you hear. The words or phrases in Task 1 are for your reference.

1. It's more digital, more _____, more mobile, more connected.
2. The company owns twelve trusted brands _____ the comfort of a city center Holiday Inn to the luxury of an Intercontinental _____.
3. They're _____ delivering high-quality service in order to keep up with the changing tastes and needs of modern travelers.
4. With nearly 744,000 _____, they provide nearly 157 million guest nights _____.
5. Intercontinental hotels group is a truly _____ company.

Task 3

Directions: *Listen to the following passage and use the sentence patterns given in Task 2 to fill in the blanks.*

___1___. It has more rooms in more places than any other hotel company. ___2___. Their guests are as varied as their brands. ___3___. Wherever you travel, you will see their hotels. As for business travel, the company believes that it should work better. ___4___. So they have properties located in major urban centers, gateway cities and resort destinations all around the globe. ___5___. The company's vision is to become one of the great companies in the world by creating Great Hotels Guests Love.

Task 4

Directions: *Listen again to the short speech in the "Reference Passage" and repeat and retell it in your own words. You will have 2 minutes for preparation.*

Section B

Task 1

Directions: *Match the questions asked at check-out with the responses.*

_____ 1. May I help you?
_____ 2. May I have your room key, please?
_____ 3. What is the extra fee for?
_____ 4. May I leave the luggage here until I finish lunch?
_____ 5. Will you be paying by cash or credit card?

a. Sure, here you are.

b. Certainly. You can leave your luggage in our storage space.

c. That is for your phone call.

d. I'd like to check out.

e. Credit card, if you accept Visa.

Task 2

Directions: *Suppose you are the receptionist and your partner will be a guest. Role-play the check-out situation with your partner. The following sample dialogue will help you finish the task. You can also make your own dialogue according to the requirements below.*

For the receptionist:

1. Offer help to the guest.

2. Ask about the key and the room number.

3. Show the guest the bill.

4. Explain that the charge is from the phone calls.

5. Offer help for the guest's luggage.

6. Say goodbye to the guest.

For the guest:

1. You need to check out.

2. Your room number is 1419.

3. You're confused about the charge.

4. You want to pay by credit card.

5. You want to leave your luggage there until you finish your lunch.

6. Thanks for their help and say goodbye.

Sample Dialogue:

Receptionist: Good morning, Sir. May I help you?

Guest: Yes, I'd like to check out.

Receptionist: May I have your room key, please?

Guest: Sure. Here you are.

Receptionist: Just a moment please. Our housekeeping need several minutes to check your room.

Unit 2 Hotel

Guest: OK.

(5 minutes later)

Receptionist: Thank you for waiting. Here is your bill.

Guest: What is this charge for?

Receptionist: Let me see... That is for your phone call.

Guest: Oh, I see.

Receptionist: Will you be paying by cash or credit card?

Guest: Credit card, if you accept Visa.

Receptionist: Sure. If everything is okay, would you sign here please?... Thank you. That's all.

Guest: By the way, may I leave the luggage here until I finish lunch?

Receptionist: Certainly, you can leave your luggage in our storage space.

Guest: Thank you very much.

Receptionist: You're welcome and have a good meal.

Part Ⅱ Writing

Task 1

Directions: *Listen to the following useful sentences or structures which can be used to write an essay.*

1. There are many factors you need to look out for when choosing a hotel.
2. Choosing a hotel is one of the most important decisions in ensuring that you have an enjoyable time.
3. Staying in this kind of hotel, I will feel comfortable, relaxed and enjoyable. That is the meaning of traveling.
4. The first aspect is... the second aspect is... the third aspect is...
5. To begin with... what's more... in addition...

Task 2

Directions: *Rank the five factors from 1 (the least important) to 5 (the most important) according to your idea on choosing a hotel.*

price   location   service   facility   review

1. _____   2. _____   3. _____   4. _____   5. _____

Task 3

Directions: *Listen to the descriptions about the five factors and match the descriptions with the right factor.*

Price: _____

Location: _____

Service: _____

Facility: _____

Review: _____

A. It is always pleasant to stay in a hotel that has a spa, several restaurants, a gym, a beauty salon, a coffee shop, a party room, a play area, a library, broadband connection, a beautiful garden and excellent function rooms.

B. It's often better to stay at the center of town where restaurants and shops are around.

C. Going to the home sites of these hotels sometimes lets you book a room directly with the owner and you get lots more information.

D. Sometimes the price isn't equal to the facilities, the service and so on.

E. The attraction is not tall buildings and good facilities to me but the heart of service.

F. There are so many sites now offering the latest reviews of hundreds of guests.

G. You can view pictures and read about amenities and facilities.

H. You save time and money as you can just walk or take a short ride to the hotel from wherever you are.

I. Spending too much money on the hotel will increase the budget that I can't afford.

Unit 2 Hotel

Task 4

Directions: *In this section, you are required to write an essay illustrating how to choose an ideal hotel within 30 minutes. The essay should be more than 150 words. The following sample writing will help you.*

Sample Writing:

My Ideal Hotel

My ideal hotel mainly includes the following several aspects.

The first aspect is the service concept. The hotel should be based on the service. The attraction is not tall buildings and good facilities to me, but the heart of service. My ideal hotel service should be attentive service, patience, compassion, wholehearted service, family service, premium(优质的) service, extension(延伸) service, zero defect service. Money is limited, but the service is unlimited and endless. The development of the hotel must be based on the high quality service.

The second aspect is the facilities. Firstly, the hotel needs to meet the guest to eat, live, entertainment. So the hotel needs to provide the perfect accommodation, catering, entertainment, conference and other places and facilities. Secondly, the hotel should have good security measures, such as fire control facilities and monitoring facilities. In addition, there should be a complete set of emergency plans.

The third aspect is the geographical location of hotel. To success for any hotel, three important factors are location, location and location. My ideal hotel not only needs to be away from the bustling(繁忙的) city, but also has convenient transportation, and it has the good ecological environment and the beauty of the scene.

This is my ideal hotel. I believe that in such an environment, I can go wholeheartedly into work and get a better day.

Unit 3 Shopping

Part Ⅰ Speaking

Section A

Task 1

Directions: *Please match the following English words and phrases with their Chinese meanings.*

_____ 1. customer satisfaction   a. 瑕疵

_____ 2. be likely to   b. 讨价还价

_____ 3. defective product   c. 染污的,弄脏的

_____ 4. at a discount rate   d. 以折扣价

_____ 5. off season   e. 在收银台

_____ 6. haggling   f. 可能

_____ 7. replace   g. 不合格产品

_____ 8. stained   h. 客户满意度

_____ 9. flaw   i. 淡季

_____ 10. at the register   j. 替换

Task 2

Directions: *Listen to the following sentences and fill in the blanks by using the*

Unit 3 Shopping

words you hear. The words or phrases in Task 1 are for your reference.

1. You can often find slightly damaged or out of season designer outfits sold _____.
2. If you plan ahead, you can save a lot of money by shopping _____.
3. Items made with higher quality materials _____ less _____ wear down.
4. They need to _____ less frequently.
5. A shirt is slightly _____.

Task 3

Directions: *Listen to the following passage and use the sentence patterns given in Task 2 to fill in the blanks.*

Bargaining, or haggling, is the age-old tradition of negotiating a price through discussion. If you shop for clothes, here're some tips.

* Shop at discount and sales stores. At such stores, __1__.
* Shop off-season. __2__. A swimsuit may be on sale in February, for example, if you live in a warm area.
* Buy secondhand clothes. Thrift stores and consignment stores are excellent means to find cheap clothing items.
* Choose quality items. __3__. Therefore, __4__.
* Ask for a discount. If you notice a zipper is broken, __5__, or some other minor flaw, try asking for a discount at the register.

Task 4

Directions: *Listen again to the short speech in the "Reference Passage" and repeat or retell it in your own words. You'll have 2 minutes for preparation.*

Section B

Task 1

Directions: *Read the following resume and answer the questions based on the given information. Act out an Interview with your partner, the questions below can be used as guidelines.*

Now you'll read an introduction.

Quality:

   Managing quality is crucial for businesses. Quality products help to maintain customer satisfaction and loyalty and reduce the risk and cost of replacing faulty goods. Your customers expect you to deliver quality products. If you do not, they will quickly look for alternatives. Besides, quality products make an important contribution to long-term revenue and profitability. They also enable you to charge and maintain higher prices.

Price:

   A business can use a variety of pricing strategies when selling a product or service. The price can be set to maximize profitability for each unit sold or from the market overall. It helps consumers to have an image of the standards the firm has to offer through their products, creating firms to have an exceptional reputation in the market. The firm's decision on the price of the product and the pricing strategy impacts the consumer's decision on whether or not to purchase the product.

Questions:

1. What's the importance of quality for a business?
2. What does good quality bring to a business?
3. How should a business set its price?
4. What's the relation between quality and price?
5. Which do you think is more important when you buy a product, quality or price?
6. Could you find some examples about products with low price and good quality?

Task 2

Directions: *Give a short speech based on your understanding of the sentence "Price has no meaning without a measure of the quality being purchased" by W. Edwards Deming. The following sample passage will help you finish the task. You can also make your own speech according to the given information in Task 1.*

Unit 3 Shopping

Sample Passage:

In today's market, Price vs Quality, which is more important?

According to a survey done in Germany, it says, price is more important than quality for the majority of Europeans when it comes to grocery shopping. Germany, France and Poland are the most price conscious nations in Europe, while the Italians clearly place a higher value on quality. These are some of the findings of GFK's European Consumer Survey 2004. No doubt that this survey is for food products but the issue is the same which is Price vs Quality.

But as a human being, we certainly believe in this statement, "Is price important, yes it is... but no price is a good price if you don't like the quality!"

Overall it is all depends on what you purchase. Some products we need really good quality and in some products price is more critical. But if price is chosen, you should never forgo quality completely.

Looking at today's world market, price is most important. People are buying things based on price. People need to save money in this hard time. First and foremost is the question of price and consumer loyalty.

Personally, I find this nonsense. It is true that for some people price is the most important factor, but not ALL people. This is simply a matter of segmentation.

(*Reference: http://www.roslihanip.com/business/price-vs-quality*)

Part II Writing

Task 1

Directions: *Listen to the following useful sentences which can be used to describe the pictures and charts.*

1. In this analysis we will examine XX pie charts.
2. (比例第二大部分)and then(比例第三大部分)are the next major expenses at X% and Y% respectively.
3. It is not surprising to find out that....
4. XX and the XXX account for nearly XX% of the total.

5. To sum up,说明三个饼图的相关含义,如无,可提炼一下每个饼图最典型的特征。

Task 2

Directions: *Here are three paragraphs which can compose the writing structure concerning how to describe the changes in the pictures or charts and state the related reasons. Decide which paragraph should be the beginning, the body and the ending.*

Paragraph one:

From these figures one can easily see that .... Many factors that contribute to the phenomenon may be summarized as follows. Above all, ... What's more,.... Last but not the least, ...

Paragraph two:

Based on the factors discussed above, all the analysis point to an unshakable conclusion. The trend does not exist in this single field, and it is bound to produce a profound influence on relevant spheres. So it is not surprising to say that ....

Paragraph three:

As we can see from the diagram, remarkable tendency that has occurred in the sphere draws our attention. The (pie) chart shows the percentage of.... The complaints on (比例最大的部分 A) ranks first, accounting for (A%) of the total. The next (two) significant expending items are (比例第二 B、三 C 部分), which are B% and C% respectively.

Beginning: _____

Body: _____

Ending: _____

Task 3

Directions: *In this section, you are required to write an essay within 30 minutes based on the given situation. The essay should be more than 150 words. The following sample writing will help you.*

Unit 3 Shopping

Situation 1:

Write a report for a university lecturer describing the information shown below.

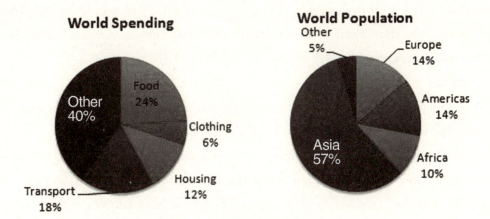

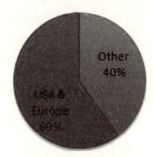

Reference Writing: *Read the following sample and pay more attention to the underlined parts in the passage which are helpful for your writing task.*

Beginning:

In this analysis we will examine three pie charts. The first one is headed "World Spending." The second is "World Population" and the third is "Consumption of Resources."

Body:

In the first chart we can see that people spend most of their income (24%) on food. In some countries this percentage would obviously be much higher. Transport and then housing are the next major expenses at 18% and 12% respectively. Only 6% of income is spent on clothing.

In the second chart entitled "World Population", it is not surprising to find that

57% of people live in Asia. In fact China and India are two of the most populated countries in the world and they are both situated on this continent. Europe and the Americans account for nearly 30% of the total, whilst 10% of people live in Africa.

Finally, the third chart reveals that the USA and Europe consume a huge 60% of the world's resource.

Ending:

To sum up, the major expenditure is on food, the population figures are the highest for Asia and the major consumers are the USA and Europe.

(Reference: http://ielts.koolearn.com/20140409/785708.html)

Situation 2: *The below data which shows the statistics of different types of complaints received by ABC Import & Export Co. Ltd. in 2016. Suppose you're in charge of the customer service center, you are required to write a report, analyzing reasons of customer complaints and giving your suggestions to your boss to reduce the complaints in the future. The essay should be more than 150 words.*

Unit 4 Banking

Part Ⅰ Speaking

Section A

Task 1

Directions: *Please match the following English words and phrases with their Chinese meanings.*

_____ 1. tuition   a. 严酷的
_____ 2. loan   b. 还清
_____ 3. debt   c. 积累社会经验
_____ 4. harsh   d. 独立的
_____ 5. pay off   e. 贷款
_____ 6. be likely to   f. 巨大的家庭开支
_____ 7. stimulate   g. 可能
_____ 8. independent   h. 学费
_____ 9. tremendous household expenditure   i. 激励
_____ 10. accumulate social experience   j. 债务

Task 2

Directions: *Listen to the following sentences and fill in the blanks by using the*

words you hear. The words or phrases in Task 1 are for your reference.

1. I choose to pay my _____ with the loan from the bank.
2. I firmly believe in the saying that "_____ life produces a diligent and intelligent man."
3. I am able to cherish my college life and have the pressure that _____ me to study hard.
4. I sometimes do part-time jobs in order to _____ the debt.
5. I don't have to rely on my parents who are always working hard on the _____.

Task 3

Directions: *Listen to the following passage and use the sentence patterns given in Task 2 to fill in the blanks.*

I am a senior college student, __1__. My decision is based on the following considerations. First of all, with the loan I can be more independent. That is to say, __2__. I can pay the tuition and support the college life completely on my own. What's more, __3__. As a result, I'm more likely to have good performance on my courses and succeed in school. Last but not least, __4__. While doing these jobs, I have accumulated a lot of social experience, which is extremely beneficial for my future career. I think the above are the advantages the loan from the bank has brought to me. __5__.

Task 4

Directions: *Listen again to the short speech in the "Reference Passage" and repeat or retell it in your own words. You'll have 2 minutes for preparation.*

Section B

Task 1

Directions: *Read the following passage about personal finance management and answer the questions based on the given information.*

Unit 4 Banking

Personal finance is the financial management which an individual or a family performs to budget, save, and spend the money in order to get beneficial reward.

There are mainly three aspects of finance products: (1) Banking products, including savings accounts, credit cards and consumer loans. (2) Investment products, such as real estate(房地产), stock market(股市), bonds(债券)and funds(基金). (3) All kinds of insurance(保险), such as life insurance, health insurance, disability insurance and so on.

The following graph shows the average data of how Chinese people arrange their money in 2015:

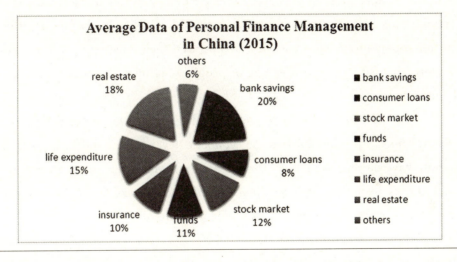

Questions:

1. What is personal finance management?
2. How did people arrange their money in the past?
3. How do people arrange their money now?
4. What do you think are the reasons for the changes?
5. What are the advantages of personal finance management?
6. Do you agree that personal finance management should be taught in schools?

Task 2

Directions: *Give a short speech based on your understanding of personal finance management. The following sample passage will help you finish the task. You can also make your own speech according to the given infor-*

mation in Task 1.

Sample Passage:

Personal Finance Management

Personal finance is the financial management which an individual or a family tries to take risks to budget, save and spend the money in order to get high returns.

The recent ten years have witnessed great changes in the ways that people arrange their finance. In the past, most people deposited their money in the bank to get a low interest. Nowadays, people invest their money in various finance products. The graph shows that in 2015 there are only 20% Chinese people who save their money in the bank. About 18% people use their money to buy houses. Life expenditure accounts for 15%, which indicates that people are more likely to enjoy their life and are not reluctant to spend money to improve their quality of living. What's more, there are also a great percentage of people who invest in stock market, insurance, funds and so on.

I think the following reasons account for the changes in personal finance management in China. First of all, with the economic development and social promotion, people now have more spare money for investment. Moreover, through internet and online platform, people receive rich financial information and form the awareness of financial management. Last but not least, people nowadays are willing to take risks and have the ability to afford potential deficit.

In my opinion, personal finance management plays a vital role in people's life. On the one hand, it enables a person or a family to perform proper investment in various areas to get a possible higher financial returns, taking into account various financial risks and future life events. On the other hand, it ensures the stable economic development of the whole society and the whole nation as well. From the above analysis, I agree that personal finance management should be taught in schools.

Part Ⅱ Writing

Task 1

Directions: *Listen to the following useful sentences which can be used to describe the*

Unit 4 Banking

pictures and charts.

1. With the development of the technological revolution, payment system has been undergoing considerable change recently.
2. As can be seen from the statistics, great changes have taken place in ...
3. There is a very sharp decline in ... in 2015 compared with that of 2010.
4. ... witnessed a dramatic increase (upward trend) in ...
5. There are many factors that may account for ... but the following are the most typical ones.
6. From the above analyses, we can draw the conclusion that ...

Task 2

Directions: *Here are three paragraphs which can compose the writing structure concerning how to describe the changes in the pictures or charts and state the related reasons. Decide which paragraph should be the beginning, the body and the ending.*

Paragraph one:

From the above analyses, we can draw the conclusion that people nowadays tend to rely on the E-payment by their cellphones to conduct personal transactions rather than the traditional way of payment. In my perspective, ...

Paragraph two:

With the development of technological revolution, payment system has been undergoing considerable change recently. As can be seen from the statistics, great changes have taken place in... The cellphone has been a platform to innovate the E-payment system, which is regarded as a new significant mode of bank industry.

Paragraph three:

According to the statistics, the five years from 2010 to 2015 have witnessed a dramatic upward trend in cellphone payment, including payment done by Alipay and Wechat. On the contrary, there is a very sharp decline in traditional payment in 2015 compared with that of 2010. Obviously, E-payment is playing an increasingly vital role in people's life. There are many factors that may account for the phenomenon but the following are the most typical ones. First of all,（理由一及简单论述）.

Moreover,(理由二及简单论述). Last but not least,(理由三及简单论述).

Beginning: _____

Body: _____

Ending: _____

Task 3

Directions: *In this section, you are required to write an essay within 30 minutes based on the given situation. The essay should be more than 150 words. The following sample writing will help you.*

Situation 1:

The following line chartshow the changes in the way people make their payment from 2010 to 2015. Read the data and share your opinions on the trends toward E-payment. You are required to write a report, emphasizing the importance of E-payment.

How People Make Their Payment

(Line chart showing: pay by cash, pay with bank cards, pay by Alipay, pay by Wechat, from 2010 to 2015, y-axis 0%–80%)

Reference Writing: *Read the following sample and pay more attention to the underlined parts in the passage which are helpful for your writing task.*

The Importance of E-payment

Beginning:

With the development of technological revolution, payment system has been undergoing considerable change recently. As can be seen from the statistics, great changes have taken place in the payment field. The cellphone has been a platform to innovate the E-payment system, which is regarded as a new significant mode of bank industry.

Unit 4 Banking

Body:

According to the statistics, the five years from 2010 to 2015 have witnessed a dramatic upward trend in cellphone payment, including payment done by Alipay and Wechat. On the contrary, there is a very sharp decline in traditional payment in 2015 compared with that of 2010. Obviously, E-payment is playing an increasingly vital role in people's life. There are many factors that may account for the phenomenon but the following are the most typical ones. First of all, E-payment provides great convenience and high efficiency. Transaction can be achieved quickly and efficiently by a mobile phone, and the operation is quite simple! Moreover, People can save a lot of time and they don't have to bring cash when they go out. As a result, people don't need to worry about the fake money. Last but not least, E-payment will generate a transaction record automatically for people to check, while traditional payment requires people to write down each transaction on a memo.

Ending:

From the above analysis, we can draw the conclusion that people nowadays tend to rely on the E-payment by their cellphones to conduct personal transactions rather than the traditional way of payment. In my perspective, E-payment will continue serving as a convenient and efficient way of payment in the years to come.

Situation 2:

Read the following data which shows the changes in the way college students pay their bills. The table divides the ways of payment into four parts, telling the different percentages in 2012 and in 2016, from which you will notice the trend of payment through cell phones. You are required to write a report on the topic of E-payment.

How College Students Pay Their Bills?			
		2012	2016
traditional way of payment	Pay by cash	48%	13%
	Pay with bank cards	38%	18%
E-payment through cellphones	Pay by Alipay	18%	65%
	Pay by Wechat	5%	68%

Unit 5 Enterprise

Part Ⅰ Speaking

Section A

Task 1

Directions: *Please match the following English words and phrases with their Chinese meanings.*

_____	1. management	a.	贸易关系
_____	2. knowledge	b.	知识
_____	3. essential	c.	管理
_____	4. experience	d.	盈利的
_____	5. risk	e.	风险
_____	6. introduce	f.	经验
_____	7. welcome	g.	有用的
_____	8. profitable	h.	必要的
_____	9. useful	j.	欢迎
_____	10. trade relations	k.	介绍

Task 2

Directions: *Listen to the following sentences and fill in the blanks by using the*

Unit 5 Enterprise

words you hear. The words or phrases in Task 1 are for your reference.

1. His knowledge and abilities to control the risks will be _____ for us to move forward.
2. We would like to show our warm _____ to our guests.
3. I'd like to take a few moments to _____ our new manager.
4. Tom has worked for over 20 years in finance department, so he has got lots of financial _____.
5. Effective management is _____ to the development of each company.

Task 3

Directions: *Listen to the following passage and use the sentence patterns given in Task 2 to fill in the blanks.*

Dear colleagues,

    I'd like to take a few moments to __1__ Jim, our new financial __2__. He's new to the company and to the area, so I'm sure we'll be able to show him a warm __3__. Jim has worked for over 20 years in finance __4__ and I know his __5__ will benefit us all. His knowledge of listed companies and his abilities to control the risks will be __6__ for us to move forward as a business.

Task 4

Directions: *Listen again to the short speech in the "Reference Paragraph" and repeat or retell it in your own words. You'll have 2 minutes for preparation.*

Section B

Task 1

Fill in the blanks with proper words and learn how to write an effective welcome speech.

| tone time audience's etiquette essential |

    Welcome speeches play an important part at any event, setting the stage and building enthusiasm and support for the speaker or event that will follow. An effective welcome speech is thorough and brief at the same time. It's also factually correct, follows proper _____ (礼仪), and immediately captures the _____ (听众的) attention. Here are the instructions for writing an effective welcome speech:

- Consider the specific event.
- Determine your _____ (语调).
- Write an outline of _____ (必要的) information.
- Organize the information in an appropriate order.
- _____ (为……计时) the speech.

Task 2

Now you'll see a welcome speech.

Welcome Speech

Ladies and gentlemen,

On behalf of Phoenix Textiles Factory, I'd like to extend you all warm welcome to our new product release conference!

With great efforts of our research and design staff, we have developed a new range of products. In the conference we will go much more into detail and let everyone see their fantastic features.

You will find these new products on display are also attractive in either price or quality. They will meet with great favor in the world market, and bring common benefits to us with a win-win situation.

I wish all the success and prosperity of your companies and hope our joint steps will go a long way in fostering mutual ties. Thank you.

Task 3

Suppose it is the first time Mr. William Washington visits your company, you are the sale manager in your company, give a welcome speech according to the main points given.

1. The size of the company
2. The history and development of the company
3. The procedures of your quality control

Unit 5 Enterprise

Part II Writing

Task 1

Directions: *Try to recite the following useful sentences which can be used to describe the pictures and charts.*

1. From the graph/data/result/information above, it can be seen/concluded/shown/estimated...
2. The graph shows the changes in the number of ... over the period from... to...
3. It can be seen from the chart that a very noticeable trend from 2000 to 2010 was...
4. As is suggested/unfolded/demonstrated/illustrated/mirrored in the above chart, with the sharp rise in the ...
5. In a word/in short/generally speaking/it is clear from the chart that, we can draw the conclusion that...

Task 2

Directions: *Here are three paragraphs which can compose the writing structure concerning how to describe the changes in the pictures or charts and state the related reasons.*

1. Beginning

As is vividly described in the..., great changes in ... have taken place in China over the past decade.

2. Body

There are ... main factors for these changes. To begin with... secondly... What's more...

3. Ending

In my view... the ways to promote the car sales are as follows...

Task 3

Direction: *In this section, you are required to write an essay within 30 minutes based on the given situation. The essay should be less than 120 words.*

Situation 1:

Suppose you are the sales manager in a car company. The below graph shows the car numbers in recent years, you want to promote the car sales in your company. Write an article based on the above graph.

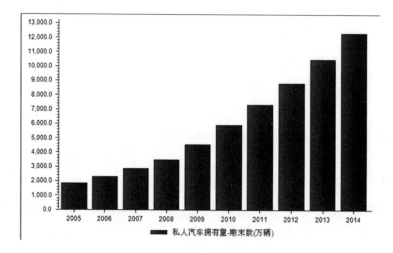

Reference Writing:

As is vividly described in the table above, great changes in car ownership have taken place in China over the past decade. The number of private cars has accordingly increased nearly 10 times from more than 14 million in 2005 to over 130 million in 2014. What's the reason? There are two main factors for these changes. To begin with, development in economy plays a vital role in these years. The higher incomes results in Chinese people's owning private cars. What's more, in modern society, time means money, many Chinese need a car to do business on time. In my view, however, the car explosion will constantly increase year by year, a large number of social problems such as traffic jams, among other things, are turning up nearly every city in China.

Situation 2:

Suppose you are the HR manager in a company. The above graph shows the educational situations in the company, you have to analyze the educational situations in your company and point out the measures on how to promote the employees' educational situations. Write an article based on the above graph.

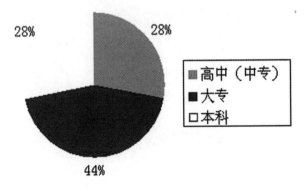

企业员工学历构成

Unit 6 Automobile

Part Ⅰ　Speaking

Section A

Task 1

Directions: *Please match the following English words and phrases with their Chinese meanings.*

_____ 1. found　　　　　　a. 标准
_____ 2. appearance　　　　b. 引擎
_____ 3. workmanship　　　c. 工艺
_____ 4. standard　　　　　d. 商标
_____ 5. brand　　　　　　e. 价格
_____ 6. engine　　　　　　f. 外观
_____ 7. performance　　　 g. 建立
_____ 8. automobiles　　　　h. 表现,性能
_____ 9. seat belt　　　　　i. 汽车
_____ 10. price　　　　　　j. 安全带

Task 2

Directions: *Listen to the following sentences and fill in the blanks by using the*

Unit 6 Automobile

words you hear. The words or phrases in Task 1 are for your reference.

1. Mazda company was _____ in 1920.
2. The automobile of this brand is famous for its high _____ of safety.
3. Buckle your _____ before you start to drive.
4. The _____ industry in China has been flourishing in recent years.
5. Most customers tend to have an appeal for the demand of _____ in purchasing.

Task 3

Direction: *Listen to the following passage and use the sentence patterns given in task 2 to fill in the blanks.*

Nowadays, automobiles play a key role in work and daily life for everyone. There are a variety of brands of cars to choose from. __1__. As a creation of modern civilization, they not only provide convenience, but also have a great contribution to economic growth. For example, Mazda is a popular brand for us. __2__. When choosing or purchasing, customers will take several factors into consideration, such as the price, the quality of comfort, after-sale service and the performance at work. __3__. Undoubtedly, people have different preferences. __4__. More importantly, please __5__.

Task 4

Directions: *Listen again to the short speech in the "Reference Passage" and repeat or retell it in your own words. You'll have 2 minutes for preparation.*

Section B

Task 1

Direction: *Read the following resume and answer the questions based on the given information. Act out an Interview with your partner, the questions below can be used as guidelines.*

Introduction

Mercedes-Benz is a German manufacturer of automobiles, buses, coaches, and trucks. The company was founded in 1900, with its headquarters in Stuttgart.

Mercedes-Benz is well-known for high standard of quality, excellent performance, technological features and incomparable comfort.

Nowadays, Mercedes-Benz has so many series, ranging from A class to S class, covering variety of utility, such as A class for family use, E class for government use, and its S class is the symbol of the luxury cars in the world. Mercedes-Benz has introduced many technological and safety innovations that help it precedents in the auto market.

Brand Name: _____   Headquartered in: _____
Product lines: _____
Product lines: 1. _____   2. _____
　　　　　　　Series & Potential Clients
　　　　　　　_____   _____
　　　　　　　_____   _____
　　　　　　　_____   _____

Questions:

1. What's the brand name of the company?
2. When was the company founded?
3. Where is the headquarters of the company?
4. What is the company specialized in?
5. Why is the company/ the brand well-known?
6. What are the series of their products?
7. How can we choose from a wide range of products?

Task 2

Directions: *Suppose you are Zhang Lu, the sales representative from the Superb Automobiles Co., LTD. Your partner will be the potential customer. Role-play to complete the dialogue. The following sample dialogue will help you finish the task. You can also make your own dialogue according to the given information in the Introduction.*

Unit 6　Automobile

Sample Dialogue:

A: Good afternoon! Welcome to our company. May I help you?

B: Good afternoon! I'd like to order a car for my wife as a gift for ten-year wedding anniversary.

A: Wow, cool! So, may I know which series of cars do you prefer, for family use or for extraordinary luxury?

B: Only as a means of transportation.

A: I see. What about price? What's your target price?

B: No more than four hundred thousand yuan. Of course, for sake of safety, I'd rather the most top-level in engine and decoration.

A: How do you think this series? It is on sales, which means a big discount and long warranty. By the way, the feedback from our customers shows that it can ensure comfortable experience and wonderful performance at work.

B: Sounds great. May I have a trial drive?

A: Of course. Please show me your ID card and driving license, I'll make it!

B: Thanks a lot!

Part II　Writing

Task 1

Directions: *Listen to the following useful sentences which can be used to describe the pictures and charts.*

1. Our products are in superb quality, as well as the performance at work.
2. The material has a durable and easy-to-clean surface.
3. The machine will pay back your investment in 6 months.
4. The model of ... is efficient and endurable, economical and practical for middle-class people.
5. The maximum speed of this kind of automobiles is ... K/H.

Task 2

Directions: *Here are three paragraphs which can compose the writing structure concerning how to describe the changes in the pictures or charts and state the related reasons. Decide which paragraph should be the beginning, the body and the ending.*

Paragraph one:

I am glad to have the opportunity to recommend to you our latest fashion style of this year.

Paragraph two:

Our products are in superb quality, as well as the performance at work. The material has a durable and easy-to-clean surface. The maximum speed of this kind of automobiles is... K/H. The model of... is efficient and endurable, economical and practical for middle-class people. We would give you a good discount on a large order. Moreover, the machine will pay back your investment in 6 months.

Paragraph three:

... are becoming indispensable in our lives. Just have a try!

Beginning: _____
Body: _____
Ending: _____

Task 3

Direction: *In this section, you are required to write an essay within 30 minutes based on the given situation. The essay should be more than 150 words. The following sample will help you.*

Situation 1

Suppose you are the sales representative in a car company. The graph below shows the sales of private cars in recent years, you want to promote the cars and make a presentation of clients' consumption motivation. Write an article based on the following graph.

Unit 6 Automobile

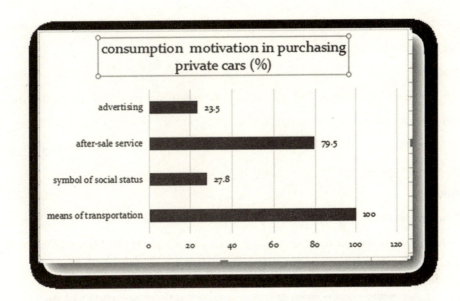

Reference Writing:

Beginning

I am glad to have the opportunity to introduce to you the sales of private cars this year. Recently, with the fantastic development of science and technology, and along with the dramatic improvement in people's living standards, families have been easily affordable for two or more private cars. From the chart, we can see the main reasons for consumers to purchase private cars is convenience in transportation, which accounts for 100%. Followed by the superb after-sale service, it assures the clients of high standard quality both in maintenance and replacement of parts. Undoubtedly, it is thought-provoking for some consumers to think of owning cars as the symbol of social status, which takes up 23.5%, the same as the proportion of advertising. Advertising will have positive effects on brand awareness.

Body

Frankly speaking, we can never imagine what our life will without private cars. The private cars do bring us more convenience than ever before. First and foremost, the private cars enable us to be more accessible and flexible to anywhere we want to go anytime. On the other hand, for sake of extraordinary comfort and superb after-sales service, people choose to take private cars for a journey nearby. Moreover, it is undoubtedly for consumers to make a purchase by impressive means of advertising.

Finally, private cars also serve as a symbol of social status, which shows us an increasingly improved standard of life.

Ending

To conclude, the spread of private cars, resulting from the dramatic development of economy and the pursuit of improved lifestyle, brought both convenience and rejoice. We will make the most of them against negative effects. Private cars are becoming indispensable in our lives. Just have a try!

Situation 2

You are the sales representative from Ford Automobile Co., LTD. You are responsible for a survey on the purchasing behavior of potential clients. You are supposed to make a report at a meeting according to the chart below.

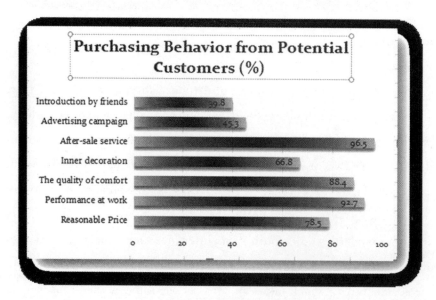

Appendix Tests

Test 1

Part Ⅰ Listening Comprehension (25 minutes)

Directions: *This part is to test your listening ability. It consists of 4 sections.*

Section A

Directions: *This section is to test your ability to give proper responses. There are 7 recorded questions in it. After each question, there is a pause. The questions will be spoken two times. When you hear a question, you should decide on the correct answer from the 4 choices marked A, B, C and D given in your test paper. Then you should mark the corresponding letter on the Answer Sheet with a single line through the center.*

Example: *You will hear*:

    You will read: A. I'm not sure. B. You're right.

                    C. Yes, certainly. D. That's interesting.

From the question we learn that the speaker is asking the listener to leave a message. Therefore, C. Yes, certainly is the correct answer. You should mark C on the Answer Sheet.

                                                        [A] [B][C] [D]

Now the test will begin.

1. A. You are late.   B. My pleasure.
   C. Go ahead, please.   D. Fine. Thanks.

2. A. Thank you.   B. I'm John Smith.
   C. Not too bad.   D. It's over there.

3. A. Pass it to me, please.   B. This way, please.
   C. Yes, of course.   D. Don't worry.

4. A. It doesn't matter.   B. Not at all.
   C. I'm fine.   D. All right.

5. A. Yes, once a month.   B. Thank you for coming.
   C. It's too late.   D. Here you are.

6. A. Mind your steps.   B. Sure.
   C. Never mind.   D. Don't mention it.

7. A. Here it is.   B. Long time no see.
   C. No problem.   D. Coffee, please.

Section B

Directions: *This section is to test your ability to understand short dialogues. There are 7 recorded dialogues in it. After each dialogue, there is a recorded question. Both the dialogues and questions will be spoken two times. When you hear a question, you should decide on the correct answer from the 4 choices marked A, B, C and D given in your test paper. Then you should mark the corresponding letter on the Answer Sheet with a single line through the center. Now listen to the dialogues.*

8. A. He forgot the time.   B. He got to the wrong place.
   C. He missed the bus.   D. He was sick.

9. A. By credit card.   B. By cheque.
   C. In cash.   D. By a gift card.

10. A. The man's work experience.
    B. The man's communication skill.
    C. The man's education background.
    D. The man's foreign language ability.

11. A. She doesn't like her job. B. She has changed her job.
    C. She has quit her job. D. She retired.
12. A. From its website. B. From its advertisement.
    C. From its newsletter. D. From its sales people.
13. A. In a supermarket. B. In a restaurant.
    C. In a hotel. D. In a hospital.
14. A. Today. B. Tomorrow.
    C. Next Monday. D. This Friday.

Section C

Directions: *In this section, there are 2 recorded conversations. After each conversation, there are some recorded questions. Both the conversations and questions will be spoken two times. When you hear a question, you should decide on the correct answer from the 4 choices marked A, B, C and D given in your test paper. Then you should mark the corresponding letter on the Answer Sheet with a single line through the center. Now listen to the conversations.*

Conversation 1

15. A. Visit a patient. B. See a doctor.
    C. Meet a friend. D. Look for a dentist.
16. A. He's got his leg broken. C. He's got a headache.
    C. He has caught cold. D. He's got a fever.

Conversation 2

17. A. Mr. Kate. B. Mr. Black.
    C. Mrs. Green. D. Mrs. Smith.
18. A. On Monday. B. On Wednesday.
    C. On Thursday. D. On Friday.
19. A. Pass a message. B. Arrange the meeting.
    C. Write a letter. D. Send an email.

Section D

Directions: *In this section you will hear a recorded short passage. The passage is printed in the test paper, but with some words or phrases missing. The passage will be read three times. During the second reading, you are required to put the missing words or phrases on the Answer Sheet in order of the numbered blanks according to what you hear. The third reading is for you to check your writing. Now the passage will begin.*

Good afternoon, ladies and gentlemen. Thank you very much for coming to our conference this afternoon. I'm Henry Johnson, the (20) _____ of Smart Toys. Now, I'd like to introduce you to a completely (21) _____ of toy manufacture. Firstly, I'll talk about the market research which led to the (22) _____ of this product. Then I'll explain the production and our sales plan. Finally, I'll make some suggestions so that you can make this product a (23) _____. We are confident this new product will sell well in the (24) _____. At the end of my speech, we'll have a question-and-answer session.

Part Ⅱ Vocabulary & Structure (10 minutes)

Directions: *This part is to test your ability to construct correct and meaningful sentences. It consists of 2 sections.*

Section A

Directions: *In this section, there are 10 incomplete sentences. You are required to complete each one by deciding on the most appropriate word or words from the 4 choices marked A, B, C and D. Then you should mark the corresponding letter on the Answer Sheet with a single line through the center.*

25. Our company's service is _____ in nearly 80 countries around the world.
    A. available   B. natural   C. relative   D. careful

26. It is the general manager who makes the _____ decisions in business.
    A. beginning   B. finishing   C. first   D. final

Test 1

27. All the traveling _____ are paid by the company if you travel on business.

    A. charges   B. money   C. prices   D. expenses

28. Ten minutes earlier, they _____ the plane.

    A. will catch   B. would catch

    C. would have caught   D. will have caught

29. When does the flight arrive in London?

    _____

    A. The departure time is 10:10.   B. The arrival time is 10:10.

    C. It leaves at 10:10.   D. It stops in Beijing at 10:10.

30. Is the flight from Shanghai on time?

    _____

    A. No, it's a direct flight.   B. No, it's delayed one hour.

    C. No, it's a two-hour flight.   D. No, it's a morning flight.

31. He _____ yesterday morning, and would stay for three days.

    A. checked   B. checked in   C. checked out   D. checking

32. An _____ charge is made for heavy bags.

    A. addition   B. in addition   C. in addition to D. additional

33. I am writing to apply for the _____ of Sales Manager advertised in yesterday's newspaper.

    A. business   B. trade   C. position   D. operation

34. John had never been abroad before, _____ he found the business trip very exciting.

    A. because   B. although   C. so   D. while

Section B

Directions: *There are also 5 incomplete statements here. You should fill in each blank with the proper form of the word given in brackets. Write the word or words in the corresponding space on the Answer Sheet.*

35. It is hard (guess) _____ what comment the manager will make on the design.

36. Payment can (make) _____ online from your checking or savings account.

37. This type of loan is (frequent) _____ used for this purpose.

38. It is possible that we reach a long-term (agree) _____ with the company.
39. I must admit that the situation is (difficult) _____ than I thought it would be.

Part Ⅲ   Reading Comprehension (35 minutes)

Directions: *This part is to test your reading ability. There are 5 tasks for you to fulfill. You should read the reading materials carefully and do the tasks as you are instructed.*

Task 1

Directions: *After reading the following passage, you will find 5 questions or unfinished statements, numbered 40 to 44. For each question or statement there are 4 choices marked A, B, C and D. You should make the correct choice and mark the corresponding letter on the Answer Sheet with a single line through the center.*

It is important for us to know how to stay safe while traveling in foreign countries. We've all heard the stories of travelers having their wallets (钱包) stolen or finding themselves in the wrong part of town. So you have to be more careful than usual, when traveling abroad.

Remember to carry a small amount of cash and a copy of your ID with you at all times. There is no need to bring large amounts of cash whit you. When shopping, use your credit card instead. Keep your wallet in your front pocket so that there is no way someone's hand could get in there without your noticing it.

Travel with a friend, business partner if possible. It is always better to travel in pairs than to go alone. Know where you're going. Look at the map before you leave the hotel so that you know where you're going and how go to there.

Lock your valuables (贵重物品) either in the safe in your hotel room or in the main hotel safe.

Be aware of your surroundings. Look around when walking, and avoid keeping your head low.

40. When shopping abroad, you are advised to _____.

    A. use online services   B. use a credit card

    C. payby check   D. pay in cash

41. To keep your wallet safe, you'd better _____.

    A. hold it in your hand   B. leave it in the hotel safe

    C. put itin your front pocket   D. keep it in your shoulder bag

42. To know where you are going, you are advise to _____.

    A. ask thepolice for detailed information

    B. look at the map before leaving the hotel

    C. always travel with your business partner

    D. have a smart phone with you while traveling

43. Where should you keep your valuables while staying in a hotel?

    A. In the hotel safe.   B. In your pockets.

    C. In your traveling bag.   D. In a beside container.

44. Which of the following can be the title for the passage?

    A. How to Ask Ways While Traveling.

    B. How to Shop in a Foreign Country.

    C. Protect Your Personal Information.

    D. Stay Safe While Traveling Abroad.

Task 2

Directions: *The following is a notice. After reading it, you will find 3 questions or unfinished statements, numbered 45 to 47. For each question or statement there are 4 choices marked A, B, C and D. You should make the correct choice and mark the corresponding letter on the Answer Sheet with a single line through the center.*

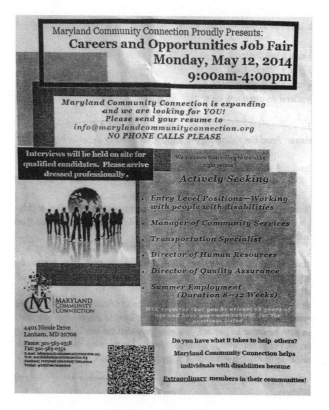

45. To apply for a position advertised, you should _____.

   A. make a phone call to the organization

   B. visit the organization in person

   C. send your resume online

   D. sign up for registration

46. When they are selected, the right persons will be _____.

   A. shown around the company   B. provided with training

   C. given a welcome party   D. sent to work abroad

47. Job candidates are advised to be dressed pressed professionally as they are likely to _____.

   A. sign a job contract   B. give a presentation

   C. help the disabled people   D. attend an interview on site

Task 3

Directions: *Read the following passage. After reading it, you should complete the*

information by filling in the blanks marked 48 to 52 (in no more than 3 words) in the table below. You should write your answers on the Answer Sheet correspondingly.

Chevron

Chevron in one of the word's leading energy companies. Our highly skilled global workforce consists of about 64,500 employees, including more than 3,200 service station employees.

In 2013, Chevron's average net production was nearly 2.6 million oil-equivalent barrels (桶) per day. About 75% of that production occurred outside the United States. Chevron had a global production of 1.96 million barrels of oil per day at the end of 2013.

We care about the environment and are proud of the many ways in which our employees work to safeguard (保护) it. Our efforts to improve on our safe work environment continue to pay off. We recognize that the world needs all the energy we can develop, in every potential form. That's why our employees work responsibly to develop the reliable energy the world needs.

Chevron
one of the world's leading energy companies

Workforce: about (48) _____ employees

Product in 2013:
  1) nearly (49) _____ oil-equivalent barrels per day
  2) about 75% of the production outside (50) _____
  3) a (51) _____ production of 1.96 million barrels of oil per day

Environment & Safety:
  1) care about the environment and safeguard it
  2) work responsibly to develop the (52) _____ the word needs

---

Task 4

Directions: *The following is a list of column titles used on a company's website. After reading it, you are required to find the items equivalent to*

(与……等同) those given in Chinese in the table below. Then you should mark the corresponding letters in order of the marked blanks, 53 through 57, on the Answer Sheet.

A — Luggage reclaim
B — office clerk
C — information desk
D — consulting director
E — underpass
F — call for assistance
G — security check
H — waiting room
I — excess baggage charge
J — boarding time
K — Don't Spit on the Floor
L — Cameras Forbidden
M — Business As Usual
N — No Admittance

Examples: (G) 安全检查　　　(I) 行李超重费

53. (	) 登机时间	(	) 认领行李
54. (	) 地下通道	(	) 办公室文员
55. (	) 打电话咨询	(	) 候车(机)室
56. (	) 请勿随地吐痰	(	) 问询处
57. (	) 闲人免进	(	) 照常营业

Task 5

Directions: Read the following letter. After reading it, you are required to complete the answers that follow the questions (No. 58 to No. 62). You should write your answers (in no more than 3 words) on the Answer Sheet correspondingly.

March 5, 2015

Dear Employees:

　　Please join me in welcoming Jim Johnson as our newest team member. Jim has become the General Manager since March 4. He will be in charge of a new project that can take our business to the national level.

　　Jim used to be the Vice President in ABC Company for the years. In that position, he looked for opportunities for improvement, made suggestions and helped make decisions.

There will be a staff lunch in the meeting room at 12:30 on March 6. Please come and introduce yourselves. Pizza and soft drinks will be provided. If you can't attend, stop by Jim's office any time next week. He will be in the new office on the second floor.

Thank you.

Best Regards,

John Davis, CEO

58. Who has joined the company?

   _____.

59. What was his position in ABC Company?

   _____.

60. What will the staff members do at the lunch party?

   They will meet the new General Manager and _____ themselves.

61. If one can't come to the lunch party, what might they do?

   They might visit the General Manager at his office any time _____.

62. Where is Jim Johnson's new office?

   It's on _____.

Part Ⅳ Translation—English into Chinese (25 minutes)

Directions: *This part, numbered 63 to 67, is to test your ability to translate English into Chinese. Each of the four sentences (No. 63 to No. 66) is followed by three choices of suggested translation marked A, B, and C. Make the best choice and write the corresponding letter on the Answer Sheet with a single line through the center. And then write your translation of the paragraph (No. 67) in the corresponding space on the Translation/Composition Sheet.*

63. Customers from various countries are warmly welcome to establish and develop business contacts in China.

   A. 在各国的中国客商都能适应当地的风俗习惯。

   B. 热烈欢迎各国客商在华建立和发展业务联系。

   C. 各国的客商在中国经商都会受到热烈的欢迎。

64. I am grateful for all the arrangement for this visit, and I enjoyed everything of it.

   A. 我对你们的这次安排深表谢意,你们组织的所有活动我都参加。

   B. 这次访问我们收获颇丰,我学到了你们的丰富经验,印象深刻。

   C. 非常感谢你们对这次访问的所有安排,每一项安排我都很满意。

65. You can try booking a flight by using your smartphone, but most airlines aren't that advanced yet.

   A. 你可以用智能手机预选座位,但大多数航空公司还未能提供这种服务。

   B. 你可以尝试用智能手机定机票,但大多数航空公司还没有这么先进。

   C. 你可以在飞行过程中使用智能手机,但是大多数航班都不允许这么做。

66. The VIP customer can take advantage of discounted room rates on a "first come, first served" basis.

   A. 贵宾们可以根据"先来先得"的原则,享受折扣房价的优惠。

   B. 本酒店按照"先来后到"的顺序安排贵宾入住并确定房价。

   C. 根据"先来后到"的原则,先来的客人可选择房价折扣率。

67. We are so sorry not to be able to accept your kind invitation to lunch on the Fourteenth. Unfortunately, our plans have been changed, and we will be returning to Hong Kong on Monday. I do hope we can have the opportunity in the near future. Janey joins me in kind regard.

   _____

   _____

   _____

Part Ⅴ Writing (25 minutes)

Directions: *This part is to test your ability to do practical writing. You are required to write a Notice according to the following instructions given in Chinese. Remember to do your writing on the Translation/Composition Sheet. The first sentence has been done for you.*

说明:以办公室名义写一份有关会议室的使用须知。

Test 1

内容如下：

1. 保持会议室整洁
2. 会后请带走您的文件和私人用品，关闭所有电器(请举例)，关闭会议室所有门窗
3. 其他注意事项(内容自加)
4. 表示感谢
5. 日期：2017年6月20日

Notice

The conference room is available to all，but we need your help to follow the rules listed below：

Test 2

Part I Listening Comprehension (25 minutes)

Directions: *This part is to test your listening ability. It consists of 4 sections.*

Section A

Directions: *This section is to test your ability to give proper responses. There are 7 recorded questions in it. After each question, there is a pause. The questions will be spoken two times. When you hear a question, you should decide on the correct answer from the 4 choices marked A, B, C and D given in your test paper. Then you should mark the corresponding letter on the Answer Sheet with a single line through the center.*

Example: You will hear:

You will read: A. I'm not sure.   B. You're right.
                C. Yes, certainly.   D. That's interesting.

  From the question we learn that the speaker is asking the listener to leave a message. Therefore, C. Yes, certainly *is the correct answer. You should mark C on the Answer Sheet.*

                                                            [A] [B][C] [D]

Now the test will begin.

Test 2

1. A. Who's calling, please? B. How are you?
   C. Where is she? D. No, you can't.
2. A. It's possible. B. That's all right.
   C. No way. D. My pleasure.
3. A. Yes, of course. B. Is it true?
   C. You're welcome. D. No, thanks.
4. A. Yes. When? B. Yes. What?
   C. Well, how? D. Well, who?
5. A. Never mind. B. Not likely.
   C. I'm afraid I can't. D. Quite well.
6. A. Just a moment, please. B. Fine, thank you.
   C. See you. D. Well done.
7. A. No problem. B. Many times.
   C. I don't know. D. My pleasure.

Section B

Directions: *This section is to test your ability to understand short dialogues. There are 7 recorded dialogues in it. After each dialogue, there is a recorded question. Both the dialogues and questions will be spoken two times. When you hear a question, you should decide on the correct answer from the 4 choices marked A, B, C and D given in your test paper. Then you should mark the corresponding letter on the Answer Sheet with a single line through the center. Now listen to the dialogues.*

8. A. Holiday food. B. Children's food.
   C. Chinese food. D. Western food.
9. A. In a bookstore. B. In a theatre.
   C. At the Customs. D. At a bank.
10. A. There is a visitor at the door.
    B. The woman is calling Jack.
    C. The door is open.
    D. The telephone is ringing.

11. A. To finish her work.　　　　　　　　B. To attend a meeting.
　　 C. To get an important paper.　　　　D. To meet somebody.
12. A. To get some medicine.　　　　　　 B. To have a check up.
　　 C. To visit a patient.　　　　　　　　D. To look after the man.
13. A. In a store.　　　　　　　　　　　　B. At a restaurant.
　　 C. At a bus stop.　　　　　　　　　　D. In a post office.
14. A. At 1:40.　　　　　　　　　　　　　B. At 1:50.
　　 C. At 2:00.　　　　　　　　　　　　　D. At 3:50.

Section C

Directions: *In this section, there are 2 recorded conversations. After each conversation, there are some recorded questions. Both the conversations and questions will be spoken two times. When you hear a question, you should decide on the correct answer from the 4 choices marked A, B, C and D given in your test paper. Then you should mark the corresponding letter on the Answer Sheet with a single line through the center. Now listen to the conversations.*

Conversation 1

15. A. To be a teacher.　　　　　　　　　B. To take care of animals.
　　 C. To work as a secretary.　　　　　 D. To further her study.
16. A. To work in an office.　　　　　　　B. To be an animal doctor.
　　 C. To go abroad.　　　　　　　　　　D. To be a salesman.

Conversation 2

17. A. She lost her data.
　　 B. She broke the disc.
　　 C. She bought a computer of a wrong model.
　　 D. She couldn't get her computer working.
18. A. Buy a computer for her.　　　　　　B. Go to the store with her.
　　 C. Lend her some money.　　　　　　 D. Replace the disc for her.

Test 2

19. A. To show the receipt. B. To call the store first.
    C. To pay some more money. D. To bring the instruction manual.

Section D

Directions: *In this section you will hear a recorded short passage. The passage is printed in the test paper, but with some words or phrases missing. The passage will be read three times. During the second reading, you are required to put the missing words or phrases on the Answer Sheet in order of the numbered blanks according to what you hear. The third reading is for you to check your writing. Now the passage will begin.*

Scientists have discovered that tea is good for us. It tastes good and it is refreshing. In recent (20)_____ studies, tea has been found to help prevent heart attacks and cancer.

One study suggests that both black tea and green tea help (21)_____ the heart. In the study, tea drinkers had a 44 percent (22)_____ death rate after heart attacks than non-drinkers. Other studies have shown that tea, like fruit and vegetables, helps fight against chemicals that may (23)_____ the development of certain cancers.

Many people really like tea. Next to plain water, it's the world's most (24)_____ drink.

Part Ⅱ Vocabulary & Structure (10 minutes)

Directions: *This part is to test your ability to construct correct and meaningful sentences. It consists of 2 sections.*

Section A

Directions: *In this section, there are 10 incomplete sentences. You are required to complete each one by deciding on the most appropriate word or words from the 4 choices marked A, B, C and D. Then you should mark the* *corresponding letter on the Answer Sheet with a single line through the center.*

25. _____ he read the book, _____ he got in it.
    A. The more; the more interesting   B. The less; the more interesting
    C. The more; the more interested   D. More; more interested

26. These regulations _____ everyone, without exception.
    A. arefamiliar with   B. are related to
    C. apply to   D. are similar to

27. I need to think about _____ I should say to the interviewer.
    A. what   B. which   C. that   D. how

28. No sooner had I got home _____ it began to rain.
    A. when   B. than   C. as   D. for

29. He _____ his luggage among hundreds of others.
    A. identified   B. found   C. thought   D. realized

30. Do not _____ me to help you unless you work harder.
    A. expect   B. hope   C. depend   D. think

31. John decided to _____ the present job in order to travel around the world.
    A. give up   B. put up   C. wake up   D. break up

32. I'll let you have an answer after _____ consideration.
    A. significant   B. deep   C. immature   D. mature

33. Talking about the weather is an easy way to _____ between strangers in Britain.
    A. cut the ice   B. burn the ice   C. break the ice D. hit the ice

34. _____ he goes out for a walk.
    A. fourtunately B. occasionally   C. surprisingly D. curiously

Section B

Directions: *There are also 5 incomplete statements here. You should fill in each blank with the proper form of the word given in brackets. Write the word or words in the corresponding space on the Answer Sheet.*

35. They perceived a stranger (wander) _____ in the garden.
36. They went into their (respect) _____ bedrooms to pack.
37. Our store (serve) _____ the community for more than 5 years.
38. If I had had enough time, I (finish) _____ my work.
39. I have enjoyed my visit very much, and would like to thank all the people (concerned) _____.

Part Ⅲ Reading Comprehension (35 minutes)

Directions: *This part is to test your reading ability. There are 5 tasks for you to fulfill. You should read the reading materials carefully and do the tasks as you are instructed.*

Task 1

Directions: *Read the following passage and make the correct choice from 4 choices marked A), B), C), D)*

When people meet each other for the first time in Britain, they say "How do you do?" and shake hands(握手). Usually they do not shake hands when they just meet or say goodbye. But they shake hands after they haven't met for a long time or when they will be away from each other for a long time.

Last year a group of German students went to England for a holiday. Their teacher told them that the English people hardly shake hands. So when they met their English friends at the station, they kept their hands behind their backs. The English students had learned that the Germans shake hands as often as possible, so they put their hands in front and got ready to shake hands with them. It made both of them laugh.

40. It is _____ if you know the language and some of the customs of the country.
    A. not useful   B. not helpful
    C. very helpful   D. very bad

41. English people usually shake hands when they _____

   A. meet every time   B. meet for the first time

   C. say goodbye to each other   D. say hello to each other

42. Usually English people don't shake hands _____

   A. when they will be away for a long time

   B. when they say "How do you do?"

   C. when they just meet or say goodbye

   D. after they haven't met for a long time

43. Which is right?

   A. German people shake hands as often as possible.

   B. English people like shaking hands very much.

   C. German people hardly shake hands.

   D. Neither English people nor Germans like shaking hands.

44. This story is about _____

   A. shaking hands   B. languages

   C. customs   D. languages and customs

Task 2

Directions: *After reading the following passage, you should make the correct choice from the four choices.*

The first people to drink tea were the Chinese because the bush grew wild all over south of their country. They liked the taste, and found that the drink refreshed (使振作) them.

People living in Europe first learned about tea growing and drinking from a book printed in Italy in 1599. The writer claimed (声称) that tea was a wonderful medicine! Although people in Europe knew about tea in 1599, it was another fifty years before the first cargo (货物) of tea from China reached Holland.

A few years later, tea was brought overland from China to Russia. The long difficult journey had to be made over mountains and across deserts.

The new drink reached England in 1657. It was sold at one of the coffee houses. Only the very people rich could afford to drink it.

45. The Chinese drank tea first because _____.

   A. the tea bush grew all over south of their country

   B. they learned it from their parents

   C. the leaves of the tea smelled good

   D. they happened to know it could be drunk

46. The Chinese liked the taste of tea because _____.

   A. the tea was a bit bitter

   B. they wouldn't be thirsty when they smelled it

   C. the drink refreshed them

   D. the tea was the only drink they liked

47. People in Europe first learned that tea was _____.

   A. a wonderful medicine   B. beautiful leaves

   C. sweet leaves   D. a flower

Task 3

Directions: *Read the following passage. After reading it, you should complete the information by filling in the blanks marked 48 to 52 (in no more than 3 words) in the table below. You should write your answers on the Answer Sheet correspondingly.*

This reminder (提示) is intended to offer guidance for using email. This is not a "how-to" document, but it is rather a document that offers advice to prevent you from being cheated or toubled by emails.

Studies show that knowledge workers spend about 20 hours a week doing email and one-third of that email is unless. Still worse, 70% of this email gets handled within six minutes of arrival and the average worker is interrupted every three minutes. As a consequence, there is a cost to our organizations. While we can't control what we receive from the outside, we can make some progress from the inside, Please read this paper and take action by following its instructions. Many thanks go to Earl Hacker (CIO, WBB Consulting, Inc.) for providing some of this information from an interest site.

Reminder of Using Email

Purpose: to prevent the user from being ___(48)___ by emails

Problems with emailing:

1. knowledge workers spend about 20 hours ___(49)___ doing email
2. one-third of that email is useless
3. 70% of this email gets handled within six minutes of ___(50)___
4. the average worker is interrupted every three minutes.

Consequence: being a ___(51)___ to organizations

What email users are advised to do:

read this paper and ___(52)___ according to the instructions

Task 4

Directions: *The following is a list of column titles used on a company's website. After reading it, you are required to find the items equivalent to (与……等同) those given in Chinese in the table below. Then you should mark the corresponding letters in order of the marked blanks, 53 through 57, on the Answer Sheet.*

A — Perfect attendance bonus   B — Performance bonus
C — Income tax   D — Overtime pay
E — Back pay   F — Pay raise
G — Pay cut   H — Pay slip
I — Weekly wage   J — Minimum wage
K — Basic wage   L — Traveling allowance
M — Annual income   N — Before-tax salary
O — Medical insurance   P — Unemployment insurance
Q — Employment injury insurance

Examples: (A)全勤奖　　　(B)绩效奖金

53. ( ) 所得税	( ) 工伤保险
54. ( ) 税前薪酬	( ) 医疗保险
55. ( ) 基本工资	( ) 年收入
56. ( ) 加班工资	( ) 出差津贴
57. ( ) 失业保险	( ) 减薪

Test 2

Task 5

Directions: *Read the following letter. After reading it, you are required to complete the answers that follow the questions (No. 58 to No. 62). You should write your answers on the Answer Sheet correspondingly.*

Dear Mr. Jenkinson,

  I am interested to see your advertisementin today's *City Daily* and would like to be considered for this position as Chief Office Secretary in your company.

  I am now working as Private Secretary to the General Manager at a manufacturing company and have a wide range of responsibilities. These include attending and taking *minutes* (记录) and interviews, dealing with callers and business emails and letters when my employer is absent, helping the new employees, as well as performing the daily office duties.

  The kind of work in your companyparticularly interests me, and I would weclome the opportunity it affords to use my foreign language abilities.

  A copy of my resume is enclosed with references you require. I hope to hear from you soon and to be given the opportunity to prove myself at an interview.

  Best regards.

Yours sincerely,
Jean Carson

58. How does the writer learn about the job wanted?

  From _____ in *City Daily*.

59. What job position is the writer applying for?

  The position as _____.

60. Where is the writer working now?

  At a _____.

61. Why is the writer particularly interested in the job?

  Because she thinks she can use her _____ abilities.

62. What is enclosed with the letter?

  A copy of the writer's _____ with reference required.

Part Ⅳ Translation—English into Chinese (25 minutes)

Directions: *This part, numbered 63 to 67, is to test your ability to translate English into Chinese. Each of the four sentences (No. 63 to No. 66) is followed by three choices of suggested translation marked A, B, and C. Make the best choice and write the corresponding letter on the Answer Sheet with a single line through the center. And then write your translation of the paragraph (No. 67) in the corresponding space on the Translation/Composition Sheet.*

63. There is other information which will help you to know more about the training school.

    A. 我们还需要其他资料,以便更好地宣传培训工作。

    B. 还有其他信息来帮助你更多地了解这所培训学校。

    C. 我们还需要其他渠道来了解这所培训学校。

64. There are some necessary steps to take for a heartfelt appreciation to be shown.

    A. 要想抒发内心的情感,必须采取一些必要的步骤。

    B. 这是必须的步骤来表达内心的欣赏。

    C. 要想表达由衷的谢意,还有几个必需的步骤要完成。

65. VR technology has the power to make these sorts of fantastical possibilities a reality.

    A. 虚拟现实技术有一种能力,可以让各种神奇的可能变成现实。

    B. 虚拟现实技术有力量让各种神奇的可能成为现实。

    C. 虚拟现实技术在现实中,有各种神秘的可能性。

66. The teacher asked us to take out one piece of paper for the quiz.

    A. 老师叫我们认真准备考试。

    B. 老师让我们拿出一张纸考试。

    C. 老师让我们在一张纸上测试。

67. If an anthropologist wanted to know what Britain was like, he would do well to take his notebook to Tesco. That's partly because it sells a third of Britain's

groceries. But it is also because Tesco's customers are made up of the wealthy, middling and poor in just the same proportions as shoppers in the country as a whole. Tesco has become big by being like Britain.

Part V   Writing (25 minutes)

V. Writing (10%)

Direction: *You are required to write a letter of complaint according to the following topics.*

Suppose you live in a room in college which you share with another student. You find it very difficult to work there because your roommate always has friends visiting and has parties in the room.

Write a letter to the Accommodation Officer at the college and ask for a new room next term. You would prefer a single room.

Test 3

Part I Listening Comprehension (25 minutes)

Directions: *This part is to test your listening ability. It consists of 4 sections.*

Section A

Directions: *This section is to test your ability to give proper responses. There are 7 recorded questions in it. After each question, there is a pause. The questions will be spoken two times. When you hear a question, you should decide on the correct answer from the 4 choices marked A, B, C and D given in your test paper. Then you should mark the corresponding letter on the Answer Sheet with a single line through the center.*

Example: *You will hear:*

You will read: A. I'm not sure. B. You're right.
C. Yes, certainly. D. That's interesting.

From the question we learn that the speaker is asking the listener to leave a message. Therefore,C. Yes, certainly is the correct answer. You should mark C on the Answer Sheet.

[A] [B][C] [D]

Now the test will begin.

Test 3

1. A. Sorry, he's not in.   B. Here you are.
   C. Try again, please.   D. Thank you.
2. A. Nice to see you.   B. See you later.
   C. No, I don't.   D. Take care.
3. A. See you next time.   B. No, thanks.
   C. You are welcome.   D. Press the button here.
4. A. Over there.   B. Yes, I do.
   C. I like Chinese food.   D. Tomorrow morning.
5. A. Never mind.   B. Certainly.
   C. Only a week.   D. My pleasure.
6. A. On the Internet.   B. She's very nice.
   C. By bus.   D. It's far away.
7. A. We are busy.   B. Take it easy.
   C. It's expensive.   D. He's very kind.

Section B

Directions: This section is to test your ability to understand short dialogues. There are 7 recorded dialogues in it. After each dialogue, there is a recorded question. Both the dialogues and questions will be spoken two times. When you hear a question, you should decide on the correct answer from the 4 choices marked A), B), C) and D) given in your test paper. Then you should mark the corresponding letter on the Answer Sheet with a single line through the center. Now listen to the dialogues.

8. A. Earth Day.   B. Mother's Day.
   C. Father's Day.   D. Thanksgiving Day.
9. A. Flight numbers.   B. Bus schedules.
   C. Banking services.   D. Office hours.
10. A. How to book a flight.   B. Where to sign the name.
    C. When to hand in the form.   D. Whom to ask for help.
11. A. From newspapers.   B. From the sales department.
    C. From magazines.   D. From the website.

12. A. The development plan. B. The market share.

    C. Sales of a new product. D. Costs of advertising.

13. A. When to get the orders. B. Where to obtain the price list.

    C. How to pay for the goods. D. Whom to contact.

14. A. It has over 500 employees. B. It was started in 1998.

    C. It has several branches. D. It is located in Beijing.

Section C

Directions: *In this section, there are 2 recorded conversations. After each conversation, there are some recorded questions. Both the conversations and questions will be spoken two times. When you hear a question, you should decide on the correct answer from the 4 choices marked A), B), C) and D) given in your test paper. Then you should mark the corresponding letter on the Answer Sheet with a single line through the center. Now listen to the conversations.*

Conversation 1

15. A. Making a sales plan. B. Preparing an annual report.

    C. Doing a market survey. D. Writing a business letter.

16. A. It costs much less. B. It saves time.

    C. Most old people like it. D. most young people like it.

Conversation 2

17. A. He has got a summer job. B. He has lost his job.

    C. He has just visited a park. D. He has been to the beach.

18. A. A sales person. B. A tour guide.

    C. A manager assistant. D. A computer programmer.

19. A. Because the salary is too low.

    B. Because she has to travel abroad frequently.

    C. Because the company is too small.

    D. Because a tour guide has to work long hours.

Section D

Directions: *In this section you will hear a recorded short passage. The passage is printed in the test paper, but with some words or phrases missing. The passage will be read three times. During the second reading, you are required to put the missing words or phrases on the Answer Sheet in order of the numbered blanks according to what you hear. The third reading is for you to check your writing. Now the passage will begin.*

Good evening, ladies and gentlemen!

First of all, I'd like to (20)_____ a sincere welcome to you all, the new comers of our company. As you know, our company is one of the top 50 companies in the country and has a history of more than 100 years. I think you must (21)_____ being a member of such a great company. But we cannot (22)_____ tradition alone. We need new employees with new knowledge and creative (23)_____.

I would like to welcome you (24)_____, and from today, let's begin to work together.

Part II Vocabulary & Structure (10 minutes)

Directions: *This part is to test your ability to construct correct and meaningful sentences. It consists of 2 sections.*

Section A

Directions: *In this section, there are 10 incomplete sentences. You are required to complete each one by deciding on the most appropriate word or words from the 4 choices marked A, B, C and D. Then you should mark the corresponding letter on the Answer Sheet with a single line through the center.*

25. The new trade figures have just been _____.

    A. removed   B. released   C. relaxed   D. relieved

26. We _____ that we will meet a certain amount of resistance to our plan.

    A. expect   B. wish   C. anticipate   D. hope

27. Fish _____ very largely in the diet of these island last year.
    A. featured   B. feature   C. fed   D. Feed
28. If you want to _____ that you catch the plane, take a taxi.
    A. sure   B. ensure   C. certain   D. enhance
29. The sum hasn't worked out, but I can't see where I _____.
    A. go bad   B. go wrong   C. go well   D. go right
30. We _____ up the windows of the old house.
    A. nailed   B. closed   C. unfold   D. open
31. The car company will be _____ its latest models at a press conference tomorrow.
    A. unveiling   B. veiling   C. unveil   D. veil
32. We waited until five o'clock, but he did not _____.
    A. show off   B. show around   C. show up   D. show along
33. These tax reforms are an attempt to _____ the gap between the rich and poor.
    A. build   B. establish   C. enhance   D. bridge
34. She _____ the top job in the automobile company.
    A. land   B. lands   C. land in   D. lands in

Section B

Directions: There are also 5 incomplete statements here. You should fill in each blank with the proper form of the word given in brackets. Write the word or words in the corresponding space on the Answer Sheet.

35. The company(establish) _____ in 1850.
36. Her speech left a deep (impress) _____ on the audience.
37. The designers from our firm are ready (assist) _____ you throughout the whole process.
38. It seems to me that his solution is much (effective) _____ than mine.
39. I'm looking forward to (meet) _____ you in Shanghai next week.

Part III Reading Comprehension (35 minutes)

Directions: *This part is to test your reading ability. There are 5 tasks for you to fulfill. You should read the reading materials carefully and do the tasks as you are instructed.*

Task 1

Directions: *After reading the following passage, you will find 5 questions or unfinished statements, numbered 40 to 44. For each question or statement there are 4 choices marked A, B, C and D. You should make the correct choice and mark the corresponding letter on the Answer Sheet with a single line through the center.*

As supplier of most of the food we eat and of raw materials for many industrial processes, agriculture is clearly an important area of the economy. But the industrial performance of agriculture is even more important than this. For in nations where the productivity of farmers is low, most of the working population is needed to raise food and few people are available for production of investment goods or for other activities required for economic growth. Indeed, one of the factors related most closely to the per capital *income* (人均收入) of a nation is the fraction of its population engaged in farming. In the poorest nations of the world more than half of the population lives on farms. This compares sharply with less than 10 per cent in Western Europe and less than 4 per cent in the United States.

In short, the course of economic development in general depends in a fundamental way on the performance of farmers. This performance in turn, depends on how agriculture is organized and on the economic environment, or market structure, within which it function. In the following pages the performance of American agriculture is examined. It is appropriate to begin with a conversation of its market structure.

40. This passage is most probably _____.

   A. a news item

B. part of an introduction of a book

C. part of a lecture

D. an advertisement

41. What is most important to agriculture is _____.

    A. its industrial performance

    B. the amount of food it produces

    C. the per capital income of farmers

    D. the production of investment goods

42. The word "this" in "But the industrial performance of agriculture is even more important than this" refers to _____.

    A. the economy as a whole

    B. the productivity of farmers

    C. the production of investment goods

    D. the provision of food and raw materials

43. The performance of farmers essentially determines _____.

    A. the size of the working population

    B. the organization of agriculture

    C. the market structure

    D. the general development of economy

44. This passage will most probably be followed by a discussion of _____.

    A. the structure of American farming population

    B. the market structure of American agriculture

    C. the various functions of American agriculture

    D. the organization of American agriculture

Task 2

Directions: *The following is a notice. After reading it, you will find 3 questions or unfinished statements, numbered 45 to 47. For each question or statement there are 4 choices marked A), B), C) and D). You should make the correct choice and mark the corresponding letter on the Answer Sheet with a single line through the center.*

Test 3

Notes: internship 实习   recommendation   推荐

45. What is advised in the poster?
    A. A language training program   B. A youth internship program
    C. A summer camp program   D. A volunteer program
46. By joining the program, the applicants will _____.
    A. improve communication skills   B. obtain a chance to go abroad
    C. gain career experience   D. get a diploma
47. How many hours will the applicants work each week?
    A. 16 hours.   B. 18 hours.
    C. 20 hours.   D. 24 hours.

Task 3

Directions: *Read the following passage. After reading it, you should complete the information by filling in the blanks marked 48 to 52 (in no more than 3 words) in the table below. You should write your answers on the Answer Sheet correspondingly.*

December 9, 2016

Dear Committee Members and Guests:

Welcome to the Energy Capital of the World-Houston, Texas! You are warmly invited to attend the Spring 2017 Meeting of the IEEE/PES Transformers Committee (变压器协会), to be held on March 7—11, 2017. It is the sincere pleasure of Tulstar Products, Inc. to be your host for the event.

The meeting will be held at the Omni Houston Hotel, located at Four Riverway, Houston, Texas (www.omnihouston.com). The hotel is located on the west side of Houston, in the Uptown Post Oak area, about 10 minutes from downtown. The group rate for guest rooms at the Omni Houston Hotel is US $139 per night (single or double rooms), with rooms reserved under the group name "IEEE Transformers". Please contact the hotel directly for room reservation (+713-871-8181) and mention our group name.

The Institute of Electrical and Electronics Engineers, Inc. (IEEE)
www.transformerscommittee.org

Invitation Letter

Date: December 9, 2016

To: (48) _____ and guests

From: The Institute of Electrical and Electronics Engineers, Inc. (IEEE)

The meeting

Name: Spring 2017 Meeting of the IEEE/PES Transformers Committee

Time: (49) _____, 2017

Host: Tulstar Products, Inc.

Location: (50) _____ Hotel

Address: Four Riverway, Houston, Texas

Guest room reservation

Group rate for guest rooms: (51) _____ per night

Group name: (52) _____

Contact telephone: +713-871-8181

Task 4

Directions: *The following is a list of column titles used on a company's website. After reading it, you are required to find the items equivalent to （与……等同）those given in Chinese in the table below. Then you should mark the corresponding letters in order of the marked blanks, 53 through 57, on the Answer Sheet.*

A — Joint venture
B — Marketing supervisor
C — Sales manager
D — Business office
E — Financial department
F — Phone operator
G — Regional sales representative
H — Quality control department
I — Personnel resources department
J — Product development department

53. (　) 财务部　　　　　　(　) 电话接线员
54. (　) 营业部　　　　　　(　) 区域销售代表
55. (　) 合资企业　　　　　(　) 人力资源部
56. (　) 市场部主管　　　　(　) 产品研发部
57. (　) 销售经理　　　　　(　) 质检部

Task 5

Directions: *Read the following letter. After reading it, you are required to complete the answers that follow the questions （No. 58 to No. 62）. You should write your answers （in no more than 3 words）on the Answer Sheet correspondingly.*

Dear Mr. Jenkinson,

　　I am interested to see your advertisement in today's *City Daily* and would like to be considered for this position as Chief Office Secretary in your company. I am now working as Private Secretary to the General Manager at a manufacturing company and have a wide range of responsibilities. These include attending and taking minutes（记录）of meeting and interview, dealing with callers and business emails and letters when my employer is absent, helping the new employees, as well as performing the daily office duties. The kind of work in your company particularly interests me, and I would welcome the opportunity it affords to use my foreign language abilities. A copy of my resume is enclosed with references you require. I hope to hear from you soon and to be given the opportunity to prove myself at an interview.

 Best Regards.

Yours sincerely,
Jean Carson

58. How does the writer learn about the job wanted?

 From _____ in the *City Daily*.

59. What job position is the writer apply for?

 The position as _____.

60. Where is the writer working now?

 At a _____.

61. Why is the writer particularly interested in the job?

 Because she thinks she can use her _____ abilities.

62. What is enclosed with the letter?

 A copy of the writer's _____ with references required.

Part Ⅳ Translation—English into Chinese (25 minutes)

Directions: *This part, numbered 63 to 67, is to test your ability to translate English into Chinese. Each of the four sentences (No. 63 to No. 66) is followed by three choices of suggested translation marked A, B, and C. Make the best choice and write the corresponding letter on the Answer Sheet with a single line through the center. And then write your translation of the paragraph (No. 67) in the corresponding space on the Translation/Composition Sheet.*

63. To serve our club members better, we continually seek opportunities to open more clubs around the world.

 A. 为了提高俱乐部成员的整体素养,我们一直以各种不同的方式为大家提供免费的培训。

Test 3

B. 为了更好地为我们俱乐部会员服务,我们不断寻找机会在世界各地开设更多的俱乐部。

C. 为了使我们俱乐部成员享受更好的服务,我们继续寻求机会与世界各地的俱乐部合作。

64. Changing jobs frequently gives you a lot of different experiences in different environments, which shows you can adapt quickly.

    A. 频繁更换工作使你在不同环境下具有众多的经验,这就表明你能很快地适应。

    B. 不同的工作让你学会更多地适应环境,积累的不同经验也会带给你更多的机遇。

    C. 经常换工作让你体验在不同环境中的许多工作感受,从而学会迅速适应环境。

65. I am grateful for all the arrangement for this visit, and I enjoyed everything of it.

    A. 我对你们的这次安排深表谢意,你们组织的所有活动我都参加。

    B. 这次访问我们收获颇丰,我学到了你们的丰富经验,印象深刻。

    C. 非常感谢你们对这次访问的所有安排,每一项安排我都很满意。

66. If you include a photo in your application while not asked for, an employer can assume you rely on your looks.

    A. 求职信通常需要附一张照片,老板会因为看过你的照片而对你产生印象。

    B. 虽然未要求在求职函中附照片,但你还是附了照片,老板就会认为你可靠。

    C. 虽没要求,如果你还是在求职信中附了照片,雇主会认为你想靠颜值取胜。

67. Apple was so named because Jobs was coming back from an apple farm, and he was on a fruitarian diet. He thought the name was "fun, spirited and not intimidating." *Fortune* magazine named Apple the most admired company in the United States in 2008, and in the world from 2008 to 2012.

Part V Writing (25 minutes)

Directions: *This part is to test your ability to do practical writing. You are required to complete an application form according to the following information given in Chinese. Remember to do your writing on the Translation / Composition Sheet.*

说明:假定你是人力资源部的员工李建新,请根据下列内容写一份加班申请表。
申请日期:2017年3月1日
部门:人力资源部(Human Resources Department)
加班时间:2017年3月5日9:00 a.m. —5:00 p.m.
总加班时间:不超过8小时
加班原因:
　　公司最近需要招聘各类员工。人力资源部一周前登了招聘广告,并已收到很多求职信(application letter)。为了协助各部门安排面试,本人需要在周六加班一天,了解应聘人员情况,并安排面试。

Overtime Request Form

Request Date:(68) _____

Employee's Name:(69) _____

Department:(70) _____

Date of Overtime: March 5, 2017

Overtime needed: from (71) _____ to 5:00 p.m.

Total Overtime: not to exceed (72) _____ hours

Reasons for Overtime Required:
_____
_____
_____

注:最后部分请写成段落。

Test 4

Part Ⅰ Listening Comprehension (25 minutes)

Directions: *This part is to test your listening ability. It consists of 4 sections.*

Section A

Directions: *This section is to test your ability to give proper responses. There are 7 recorded questions in it. After each question, there is a pause. The questions will be spoken two times. When you hear a question, you should decide on the correct answer from the 4 choices marked A, B, C and D given in your test paper. Then you should mark the corresponding letter on the Answer Sheet with a single line through the center.*

Example: *You will hear*:

    You will read: A. I'm not sure.   B. You're right.

                    C. Yes, certainly.   D. That's interesting.

From the question we learn that the speaker is asking the listener to leave a message. Therefore, C. Yes, certainly *is the correct answer. You should mark C on the Answer Sheet.*

                                                           [A] [B][C] [D]

Now the test will begin.

1. A. Sure.　　　　　　　　　　　B. I have no idea.
   C. It's far from here.　　　　　　D. Sorry, I have forgotten.
2. A. How nice!　　　　　　　　　B. Not at all.
   C. That's nothing.　　　　　　　D. me, too.
3. A. She likes singing.　　　　　　B. She likes to travel.
   C. She looks sad.　　　　　　　 D. She looks much like her mother.
4. A. For one week.　　　　　　　 B. Twice a week.
   C. Since last week.　　　　　　　D. The day after tomorrow.
5. A. No, it's not mine.　　　　　　B. Yes, here you are.
   C. Sorry, I can't hear you clearly.　D. Ask Tom, please.
6. A. ＄2500.　　　　　　　　　　B. 2500kg.
   C. 2500 km.　　　　　　　　　　D. 2500 a pair.
7. A. Hold on, please.　　　　　　　B. Who are you?
   C. It's wonderful.　　　　　　　 D. It's my fault.

Section B

Directions: This section is to test your ability to understand short dialogues. There are 7 recorded dialogues in it. After each dialogue, there is a recorded question. Both the dialogues and questions will be spoken two times. When you hear a question, you should decide on the correct answer from the 4 choices marked A, B, C and D given in your test paper. Then you should mark the corresponding letter on the Answer Sheet with a single line through the center. Now listen to the dialogues.

8. A. Give a message to Mr. Johnson.　　B. Wait for Mr. Johnson.
   C. Write a note to Mr. Johnson.　　　D. Keep Mr. Johnson's note.

9. A. In a post office.　　　　　　　　B. In a florist's.
   C. In a market.　　　　　　　　　 D. On a train.
10. A. July.　　　　　　　　　　　　B. September.
    C. August.　　　　　　　　　　　D. Both July and September.
11. A. In a restaurant.　　　　　　　　B. At home.
    C. In a shop.　　　　　　　　　　D. On a train.

Test 4

12. A. By underground. B. By bus.
    C. By car. D. By bike.
13. A. They planned to go shopping.
    B. They planned to buy a football.
    C. They planned to play a football game outdoors.
    D. They planned to put off a football game.
14. A. Half. B. Four-fifths.
    C. One-fifth. D. Fifth-one.

Section C

Directions: *In this section, there are 2 recorded conversations. After each conversation, there are some recorded questions. Both the conversations and questions will be spoken two times. When you hear a question, you should decide on the correct answer from the 4 choices marked A, B, C and D given in your test paper. Then you should mark the corresponding letter on the Answer Sheet with a single line through the center. Now listen to the conversations.*

Conversation 1

15. A. Stop the car. B. Start the car.
    C. Check behind him. D. Look for a seat belt.
16. A. Check behind him. C. Start the car.
    C. Look for a seat belt. D. Fasten the seat belt.

Conversation 2

17. A. Mrs. Simpson. B. Mr. Sipson.
    C. Mr. Simpson. D. Mrs. Smith.
18. A. Next Friday afternoon. B. Next Friday noon.
    C. Friday afternoon. D. Next Friday morning.
19. A. 68742519. B. 68745219.
    C. 86475219. D. 54789651.

Section D

Directions: *In this section you will hear a recorded short passage. The passage is printed in the test paper, but with some words or phrases missing. The passage will be read three times. During the second reading, you are required to put the missing words or phrases on the Answer Sheet in order of the numbered blanks according to what you hear. The third reading is for you to check your writing. Now the passage will begin.*

While automobiles are a (20) _____ part of any transportation system, car culture makes it difficult to create sustainable urban transport. When (21) _____ demand calls for size and (22) _____ —not mobility or sustainability—(23) _____ efficiency is quickly sacrificed. Moreover, when cars become so (24) _____ valued rather than simply functionally important, necessary reforms for sustainable transport become difficult.

Part II Vocabulary & Structure (10 minutes)

Directions: *This part is to test your ability to construct correct and meaningful sentences. It consists of 2 sections.*

Section A

Directions: *In this section, there are 10 incomplete sentences. You are required to complete each one by deciding on the most appropriate word or words from the 4 choices marked A, B, C and D. Then you should mark the corresponding letter on the Answer Sheet with a single line through the center.*

25. I _____ a camera two weeks ago but I haven't had a chance to use it.
    A. have bought   B. bought   C. will buy   D. would buy

26. It's _____ interesting program and it tells us how to play _____ piano.
    A. a; the   B. an; the   C. the; a   D. the; an

27. On Fridays, I often _____ with my sister and watch *Running Man* at home.
    A. show up   B. come up   C. stay up   D. play up

Test 4

28. Something _____ in our hometown since 2014. Now it _____ very modern.
    A. is changed; is looked   B. has changed; looks
    C. changed; looks   D. changed; is looked

29. All the students in the classroom do their homework _____.
    A. enough careful   B. careful enough
    C. carefully enough D. enough carefully

30. You get wet all over. It must be raining _____ outside.
    A. heavily   B. hardly   C. carefully   D. loudly

31. In order to make Dandong more beautiful, more trees and flowers _____ every year.
    A. will plant
    B. should plant
    C. should be planted
    D. must plant

32. Tom will be able to find the hotel, he has a pretty good _____ of direction.
    A. idea   B. feeling   C. experience   D. sense

33. Father's Day is on the _____ Sunday in June. It's on June 21st this year.
    A. first   B. second   C. third   D. fourth

34. The world's population is growing _____ and there is _____ land and water for growing rice.
    A. more; less   B. larger; fewer
    C. larger; less   D. more; fewer

Directions: There are also 5 incomplete statements here. You should fill in each blank with the proper form of the word given in brackets. Write the word or words in the corresponding space on the Answer Sheet.

35. They went to have their dinner after they _____ (finish) the assignment.

36. "I _____ (see) the film. It is really worth seeing," my sister told me on the phone.

37. This means of communication _____ (be) much more effective.

38. The data he has collected _____ (be) useful to our research.

39. _____ (early) you start, the _____ (soon) you'll finish the work.

Part Ⅲ Reading Comprehension (35 minutes)

Directions: *This part is to test your reading ability. There are 5 tasks for you to fulfill. You should read the reading materials carefully and do the tasks as you are instructed.*

Task 1

Directions: *After reading the following passage, you will find 5 questions or unfinished statements, numbered 40 to 44. For each question or statement there are 4 choices marked A, B, C and D. You should make the correct choice and mark the corresponding letter on the Answer Sheet with a single line through the center.*

　　Most things cannot be enjoyed without friends, but reading can. While sitting alone in our house, we can travel around the whole world, and we can come to understand thousands of things.

　　We can also talk with the people living thousands of years ago. Though we may not be great, we can become the friends of bright men. Only books can give us these pleasant things. Some people can't enjoy them, and they are poor men; some enjoy them most and they get the most happiness from them.

40. The best topic for this passage is _____.

　　A. Books　　　　B. Reading　　C. Happiness　　D. Greatness

41. When a person is reading, he usually _____.

　　A. stays at home　　　　　　　B. sits by himself

　　C. travels around　　　　　　　D. talks with others

42. Through reading we get to know the world is _____.

　　A. too wonderful　　B. so colorful　　C. quite strange　　D. very small

43. Books help us to learn the things before us, around us and far away from us, so we might _____.

　　A. become great people　　　　B. get cleverer than before

　　C. talk with those dead persons.　D. become the friends of bright men

Test 4

44. What does a poor man mean in this passage?

   A. A person without money.
   B. A person without books.
   C. A person without friends.
   D. A person unable to enjoy reading.

Task 2

Directions: *The following is a notice. After reading it, you will find 3 questions or unfinished statements, numbered 45 to 47. For each question or statement there are 4 choices marked A, B, C and D. You should make the correct choice and mark the corresponding letter on the Answer Sheet with a single line through the center.*

On deciding to buy your first home, you're likely to be excited and full of enthusiasm(热情). However, you should take care to plan well and understand the process to avoid any unexpected problems.

Here are some things you'll need to consider to help you get started.

First, think about what you need and what you want from your new home. Perhaps you need to be close to your place of work because you don't drive. It may be that you want a large garden to satisfy your gardening hobby. Be sure to understand the differences between needs and wants as it's likely you'll need to give up some of your wants.

Then, use the internet, your local library and your friends and family to find out all you can about the buying process. You'll need to make decisions down the line and it will help if you understand the buying process.

At this stage, you will normally need to contact a mortgage(按揭)advisor to see how much money you can borrow.

Of course, there are lots of costs related to buying a home which may not be immediately clear to first time buyers.

45. If you want to buy your first home, you are advised to _____.

   A. borrow some money from a bank
   B. save enough money in advance
   C. understand the buying process
   D. get to know the housing agent

46. When buying a new home, the first thing you should consider is _____.

   A. the size of the garden
   B. your needs and wants

C. your job and income   D. the environment

47. The purpose of contacting a mortgage advisor is _____.

   A. to see whether the price of the home is reasonable

   B. to ask about the legal issues related to the buying

   C. to make sure you understand the buying process

   D. to find out how much money you can borrow

Task 3

Directions: *Read the following passage. After reading it, you should complete the information by filling in the blanks marked 48 to 52 (in no more than 3 words) in the table below. You should write your answers on the Answer Sheet correspondingly.*

Real World & Real Learning
IMD INTERNATIONAL-EXECUTIVE MBA

Focused on general management, strategy and leadership, IMD is one of the world's top ranked business schools. It's the right place for someone looking for an accurate learning experience to build on an already successful career.

Keep Your Job While Getting Your MBA. Our program is of flexibility, designed to suit the demands of fast-moving international executives. There are 18 weeks of face-to-face learning that you can spread out over whatever time period suiting you.

Broaden Your Horizon. Work closely with excellent managers from all over the world, every industry and every part of business. Deal with issues that you've never felt confident of before. Visit and explore some of the world's most exciting places for doing business. Learn how to learn.

Build Your Career. The company-focused projects you do with us will bring value to your organization, build your reputation further and give you the confidence to take on new challenges.

IMD INTERNATIONAL-EXECUTIVE MBA

Aims: for people seeking (48) _____ to establish their winning professional lives.

Features of IMD's programs: flexible and fit for busy managers who are (49) _____.

Learning time: whenever students feels (50) _____.

Way of study: together with (51) _____.

Objective of the projects: to make people feel more (52) _____ to face new tasks.

Task 4

Directions: *The following are some expressions in business. After reading it, you are required to find the items equivalent to (与……等同) those given in Chinese in the table below. Then you should mark the corresponding letters in order of the marked blanks, 53 through 57, on the Answer Sheet.*

A — CDO(Chief Development Officer)

B — CEO(Chief Executive Officer)

C — CFO(Chief Finance Officer)

D — CHRO(Chief Human Resource Officer)

E — CMO(Chief Marketing Officer)

F — CNO(ChiefNegotiation Officer)

G — COO(Chief Operation Officer)

H — CSO(Chief Sales Officer)

I — CQCO(Chief Quality Control Officer)

J — CRO(Chief Research Officer)

K — CTO(Chief Technology Officer)

L — CVO(Chief Valuation Officer)

Examples：（G）首席运营官　　　（H）销售总监

53. (	) 质控总监	(	) 开发总监
54. (	) 首席谈判代表	(	) 财务总监
55. (	) 首席人力资源总监	(	) 研究总监
56. (	) 市场总监	(	) 首席执行官
57. (	) 评估总监	(	) 首席技术官

Task 5

Directions：*The following is an advertisement. After reading it, you are required to complete the answers that follow the questions（No. 58 to No. 62）. You should write your answers（in no more than 3 words）on the Answer Sheet correspondingly.*

Ibas—Center of Excellence

Ibas is one of the world's leading companies in Data Recovery. We recover, erase（抹去）and investigate your data in a professional manner. The head office is located in Norway with subsidiaries（子公司）,distributors and partners worldwide. Lost data? Don't panic（震惊）! Ibas can help you!

　We recover your data!

With thirty years' experience in data recovery we know your problem. Choose our British-based data recovery services for situations where data seems lost. Our experienced engineers are ready to help you：call 0800 389 3818.

　We know from 25 years of experience that：

　Hard disks crash!

　Backup（辅助）systems fail!

　RAID systems fail!

　Human errors occur!

　—but there is a solution!

　Ibas recovers data from all operating systems and storage media!

58. What kind of organization is Ibas?

　It is an international company in _____.

59. Where is Ibas' services based?

   It has its services based in _____.

60. Who needs the help of Ibas?

   Anyone who _____.

61. When was Ibas set up?

   About _____ ago.

62. Who can help you if your hard disk crashes?

   _____.

Part Ⅳ Translation—English into Chinese (25 minutes)

Directions: *This part, numbered 63 to 67, is to test your ability to translate English into Chinese. Each of the four sentences (No. 63 to No. 66) is followed by three choices of suggested translation marked A, B, and C. Make the best choice and write the corresponding letter on the Answer Sheet with a single line through the center. And then write your translation of the paragraph (No. 67) in the corresponding space on the Translation/Composition Sheet.*

63. Being a car salesman is not the career choice of many people although it can be fulfilling.

   A. 尽管汽车销售员这份工作会是令人满意的,但很多人都不会把它作为事业的选择。

   B. 尽管这份工作会是令很多人满意的,但汽车销售员却不会把它作为事业的选择。

   C. 尽管这份工作会是令人满意的,但汽车销售员都不会把它作为事业的选择。

64. Cars.com offers easy-to-understand information to help you decide what car to buy and how much to pay.

   A. Cars.com 提供的信息容易理解,能帮助你决定该买什么车和花多少钱。

   B. Cars.com 列出的信息都很容易获取,并且告诉你要花多少钱买汽车。

   C. Cars.com 销售的汽车都很容易驾驶,并且允许购车者办理分期付款。

65. When you start selling cars for a car dealership, they typically provide some basic car sales training to get you started in the right direction.

   A. 当你开始在车行销售汽车时,他们会特地提供一些基本车型销售培训让你渐入轨道。

   B. 当你开始在汽车经销店销售汽车时,他们肯定会挑选一些基本汽车销售培训让你慢慢适应。

   C. 当你开始在车行销售汽车时,他们会特地挑选一些基本车型销售培训让你渐入佳境。

66. Without a car most people feel that they are poor, and even if a person is poor, he doesn't feel really poor when he has a car.

   A. 没有汽车大多数人觉得他们很穷;而且一个人即使是真的很穷,一旦有了汽车也不会觉得自己穷。

   B. 大多数人如果没有车子会以为很穷;如果有了车,尽管穷他也会觉得自己很富。

   C. 没有车时大多数人觉得自己是贫穷的;而尽管一个人是穷的,他也不会觉得穷,当他有辆车时。

67. Today's cars are already built with a kind of converter(转换器). When exhaust flows through this converter "box", a chemical inside breaks down the car's pollutants(污染物质) into less harmful chemicals. But some pollutants still escape into the air to form smog(雾), which can burn your eyes, nose and throat, and make breathing painful.

   _____
   _____
   _____

Part V Writing (25 minutes)

Directions: This part is to test your ability to do practical writing. You are required to complete a resume according to the following information given in Chinese. Remember to do your writing on the Translation/Composition Sheet.

说明：将所有信息填入下面的简历中。

李梦华，女，生于 1995 年 8 月 19 日。家住东海市滨州大道 158 号，联系电话：18654789652，电子邮箱：limenghua@126.com。

2012 年 9 月至 2016 年 7 月就读于东海大学，主修汽车营销与策划，2013 年考取驾照。曾获得 2015、2016 年度奖学金，并于 2016 年获得大学英语六级和计算机二级证书。2015 年 9 月至今在宝马 4S 店实习。

Words for reference：

奖金 scholarship

汽车营销与策划 automobile marketing and planning

实习 internship

证书 certificate

Resume

Name：(1) _____

Sex：(2) _____

Date of Birth：(3) _____

Address：158 Binzhou Avenue，Donghai

Mobile phone：(4) _____

E-mail：limenghua@126.com

Educational background：

(5) _____

_____

_____

_____

Work experience：

(6) _____

_____

_____

_____

参考答案及听力原文

Key to Unit 1

Part Ⅰ Speaking

Section A

Task 1

1~5 f j d h g   6~10 b c e i a

Task 2

1. sincerely 2. experience 3. luxurious 4. landscapes 5. On behalf of

Task 3

1. On behalf of the company and my colleagues, I'd like to extend a warm welcome to all of you.

2. I'll do everything possible to make your visit a pleasant experience.

3. You're going to stay at the May Flower, a luxurious five-star hotel.

4. You can easily visit the scenic spots and enjoy the natural and cultural landscapes around us.

5. I sincerely hope you will enjoy your stay in our city.

Task 4

(omitted)

参考答案及听力原文

Section B

Task 1

1. Her name is Li Lu.
2. She is married.
3. She graduated from Shanghai Institute of Foreign Languages and majored in tourism.
4. She wants to work as a tour guide with Suzhou International Travel Agency.
5. During the year 2014－2016, she worked as a guide for Hangzhou International Travel Service.
6. She received a tourist guide qualification certificate.

Task 2

(omitted)

Part Ⅱ Writing

Task 2

Beginning: Paragraph three

Body: Paragraph two

Ending: Paragraph one

Task 3

(omitted)

Script for Listening Comprehension

Part Ⅰ Speaking

Section A

Task 2

Directions: *Listen to the following sentences and fill in the blanks by using the words you hear. The words or phrases in Task 1 are for your reference.*

1. I sincerely hope you will enjoy your stay in our city.
2. I'll do everything possible to make your visit a pleasant experience.
3. You're going to stay at the May Flower, a luxurious five-star hotel.

4. You can easily visit the scenic spots and enjoy the natural and cultural landscapes around us.

5. On behalf of the company and my colleagues, I'd like to extend a warm welcome to all of you.

Task 3

Directions: *Listen to the following passage and use the sentence patterns given in Task 2 to fill in the blanks.*

Good morning, everyone! I'm Lisa and I'm from Shanghai Youth Travel Service Company. On behalf of the company and my colleagues, I'd like to extend a warm welcome to all of you. During your stay in our city, I will be your local guide. I'll do everything possible to make your visit a pleasant experience. If you have any problems or request, please don't hesitate to let me know. You're going to stay at the May Flower, a luxurious five-star hotel. Although the hotel is not exactly in downtown, it is strategically located with easy access to many tourist attractions. You can easily visit the scenic spots and enjoy the natural and cultural landscapes around us. As you'll be staying in our city for five days, please do remember the number of our bus. I sincerely hope you will enjoy your stay in our city.

Part Ⅱ　Writing

Task 1

Directions: *Listen to the following useful sentences which can be used to describe the pictures and charts.*

1. It is reported that in recent years several new holiday habits have been developed.

2. Based on the report we can see that in 1998, 41 percent of people stayed at home to enjoy their holidays.

3. But now the proportion has reduced to 10 percent.

4. The proportion of camping and traveling abroad was increasing steadily.

5. In short, nowadays, people's living standard has been rising greatly.

参考答案及听力原文

Key to Unit 2

Part Ⅰ Speaking

Section A

Task 1

1~5 b f e g a   6~10 i j h d c

Task 2

1. flexible   2. ranging from, resort   3. committed to   4. guest rooms; per year
5. global

Task 3

1. Intercontinental hotels group is a truly global company.
2. With nearly 744,000 guest rooms, they provide nearly 157 million guest nights per year.
3. The company owns twelve trusted brands ranging from the comfort of a city center Holiday Inn to the luxury of an Intercontinental resort.
4. They're committed to delivering high-quality service in order to keep up with the changing tastes and needs of modern travelers.
5. It's more digital, more flexible, more mobile, more connected.

Task 4

(omitted)

Section B

Task 1

1~5 d a c b e

Task 2

(omitted)

Part Ⅱ Writing

Task 2

(open)

95

Task 3

Price: D I

Location: B H

Service: E

Facility: A

Review: C F G

Task 4

(open)

Script for Listening Comprehension

Part Ⅰ　Speaking

Section A

Task 2

Directions: *Listen to the following sentences and fill in the blanks by using the words you hear. The words or phrases in Task 1 are for your reference.*

1. It's more digital, more flexible, more mobile, more connected.
2. The company owns twelve trusted brands ranging from the comfort of a city center Holiday Inn to the luxury of an Intercontinental resort.
3. They're committed to delivering high-quality service in order to keep up with the changing tastes and needs of modern travelers.
4. With nearly 744,000 guest rooms, they provide nearly 157 million guest nights per year.
5. Intercontinental hotels group is a truly global company.

Task 3

Directions: *Listen to the following passage and use the sentence patterns given in Task 2 to fill in the blanks.*

　　Intercontinental hotels group is a truly global company. It has more rooms in more places than any other hotel company. With nearly 744,000 guest rooms, they provide nearly 157 million guest nights per year. Their guests are as varied as their brands. The company owns twelve trusted brands ranging from the comfort of a city center Holiday Inn to the luxury of an Intercontinental resort. Wherever you travel, you will see their hotels. As for business travel, the company believes that it should work better. They're committed to delivering high-quality service in order to keep up with the changing tastes and needs of modern travelers. So they have properties located in major urban centers, gateway cities and resort destinations all around the globe. It's more digital, more flexible, more mobile, more connected. The company's vision is to become one of the great companies in the world by creating Great Hotels Guests Love.

Part II Writing

Task 1

Directions: *Listen to the following useful sentences which can be used to describe the pictures and charts.*

1. There are many factors you need to look out for when choosing a hotel.
2. Choosing a hotel is one of the most important decisions in ensuring that you have an enjoyable time.
3. Staying in this kind of hotel, I will feel comfortable, relaxed and enjoyable. That is the meaning of traveling.
4. The first aspect is... the second aspect is... the third aspect is...
5. To begin with... what's more... in addition...

Task 3

Directions: *Listen to the descriptions about the five factors and match the descriptions with the right factor.*

It is always pleasant to stay in a hotel that has a spa, several restaurants, a gym, a beauty salon, a coffee shop, a party room, a play area, a library, broadband connection, a beautiful garden and excellent function rooms.

It's often better to stay at the center of town where restaurants and shops around.

Going to the home sites of these hotels sometimes lets you book a room directly with the owner and you get lots more information.

Sometimes the price isn't equal to the facilities, the service and so on.

The attraction is not tall buildings and good facilities to me, but the heart of service.

  There are so many sites now offering the latest reviews of hundreds of guests.

  You can view pictures and read about amenities and facilities.

  You save time and money as you can just walk or take a short ride to the hotel from wherever you are.

  Spending too much money on the hotel will increase the budget that I can't afford.

Key to Unit 3

Part Ⅰ   Speaking

Section A

Task 1

1~5 h f g d i   6~10 b j c a e

Task 2

1. at a discount rate   2. off season   3. are likely to   4. be replaced   5. stained

Task 3

1. you can often find slightly damaged or out of season designer outfits sold at a discount rate.

2. If you plan ahead, you can save a lot of money by shopping off season.

3. Items made with higher quality materials are less likely to wear down.

4. ... they need to be replaced less frequently.

5. ... a shirt is slightly stained.

Task 4

(omitted)

Section B

Task 1

(open)

Task 2

(omitted)

参考答案及听力原文

Part II Writing

Task 2

Beginning: Paragraph one

Body: Paragraph three

Ending: Paragraph two

Task 3

(open)

Script for Listening Comprehension

Part I Speaking

Section A

Task 2

Directions: *Listen to the following sentences and fill in the blanks by using the words you hear. The words or phrases in Task 1 are for your reference.*

1. You can often find slightly damaged or out of season designer outfits sold at a discount rate.
2. If you plan ahead, you can save a lot of money by shopping off season.
3. Items made with higher quality materials are less likely to wear down.
4. They need to be replaced less frequently.
5. A shirt is slightly stained.

Task 3

Directions: *Listen to the following passage and use the sentence patterns given in Task 2 to fill in the blanks.*

Bargaining, or haggling, is the age-old tradition of negotiating a price through discussion. If you shop for clothes, here're some tips.

1. Shop at discount and sales stores. At such stores, you can often find slightly damaged or out of season designer outfits sold at a discount rate.
2. Shop off-season. If you plan ahead, you can save a lot of money by shopping off season. A swimsuit may be on sale in February, for example, if you live in a warm area.
3. Buy secondhand clothes. Thrift stores and consignment stores are excellent means

to find cheap clothing items.

4. Choose quality items. Items made with higher quality materials are less likely to wear down. Therefore, they need to be replaced less frequently.

5. Ask for a discount. If you notice a zipper is broken, a shirt is slightly stained, or some other minor flaw, try asking for a discount at the register.

Part Ⅱ　Writing

Task 1

Directions: *Listen to the following useful sentences which can be used to describe the pictures and charts.*

1. In this analysis we will examine XX pie charts.

2. ...and then...are the next major expenses at X% and Y% respectively.

3. It is not surprising to find that. ...

4. XX and XXX account for nearly XX% of the total, ...

5. To sum up, ...

Key to Unit 4

Part Ⅰ　Speaking

Section A

Task 1

1~5　h e j a b　6~10　g i d f c

Task 2

1. tuition

2. harsh

3. stimulate

4. pay off

5. tremendous household expenditure

Task 3

1. I choose to pay my tuition with the loan from the bank.

2. I don't have to rely on my parents who are always working hard on the tremen-

dous household expenditure.
3. I am able to cherish my college life and have the pressure that stimulate me to study hard.
4. I sometimes do part-time jobs in order to pay off the debt.
5. I firmly believe in the saying that "harsh life produces a diligent and intelligent man."

Task 4

(omitted)

Section B

Task 1

(open)

Task 2

(omitted)

Part Ⅱ Writing

Task 2

Beginning: Paragraph two

Body: Paragraph three

Ending: Paragraph one

Task 3

How College Students Pay Their Bills

With the development of technological revolution, ways of payment have been undergoing fundamental change in recent years. College students, for instance, pay their bills with cell phones instead of using cash. That is to say, E-payment plays an increasingly significant role in the life of college students.

As can be seen from the data in the table, great changes have taken place in payment ways of college students. According to the statistics, the four years from 2012 to 2016 have witnessed a dramatic upward trend in E-payment, such as payment done by Wechat and Alipay. However, there is a very sharp decline in payment with cash and bank cards. There are many factors that may account for those changes but the following are the most typical ones. First of all, it is easy and convenient for college students to make payment with cell phones without carrying too much cash. What's more, parents can make remote payment for their children or transfer money through cell phones without going to a bank. Finally, students can check the electronic bills to manage budgets and keep accounts.

From the above analysis, we can draw the conclusion that E-payment plays a crucial part in college students' life. As a college student, I will take full advantage of E-payment to make my life wonderful.

Script for Listening Comprehension

Part Ⅰ   Speaking

Task 2

Directions: *Listen to the following sentences and fill in the blanks by using the words you hear. The words or phrases in Task 1 are for your reference.*

1. I choose to pay my tuition with the loan from the bank.
2. I firmly believe in the saying that "harsh life produces a diligent and intelligent man."
3. I am able to cherish my college life and have the pressure that stimulates me to study hard.
4. I sometimes do part-time jobs in order to pay off the debt.
5. I don't have to rely on my parents who are always working hard on the tremendous household expenditure.

Task 3

Directions: *Listen to the following passage and use the sentence patterns given in Task 2 to fill in the blanks.*

I am a senior college student; I choose to pay my tuition with the loan from the bank. My decision is based on the following considerations. First of all, with the loan I can be more independent. That is to say, I don't have to rely on my parents who are always working hard on the tremendous household expenditure. I can pay the tuition and support the college life completely on my own. What's more, I am able to cherish my college life and have the pressure that stimulates me to study hard. As a result, I'm more likely to have good performance on my courses and succeed in school. Last but not least, I sometimes do part-time jobs in order to pay off the debt. While doing these jobs, I have accumulated a lot of social experience, which is extremely beneficial for my future career. I think the above are the advantages the loan from the bank has brought to me. I firmly believe in the saying that "harsh life produces a diligent and intelligent man."

Part Ⅱ Writing

Task 1

Directions: *Listen to the following useful sentences which can be used to describe the pictures and charts.*

1. With the development of technological revolution, payment system has been undergoing considerable change recently.
2. As can be seen from the statistics, great changes have taken place in ...
3. There is a very sharp decline in ... in 2015 compared with that of 2010.
4. ... witnessed a dramatic increase (upward trend) in ...
5. There are many factors that may account for ... but the following are the most typical ones.
6. From the above analyses, we can draw the conclusion that ...

Key to Unit 5

Part Ⅰ Speaking

Section A

Task 1

1~5 c b h f e   6~10 k j d g a

Task 2

1. useful   2. welcome   3. introduce   4. experience   5. essential

Task 3

1. introduce   2. manager   3. welcome   4. department   5. experience

6. essential

Task 4

(omitted)

Section B

Task 1

1. etiquette 2. audience's 3. tone 4. essential 5. time

Task 2

(omitted)

Part Ⅱ Writing

Task 3

(open)

Script for Listening Comprehension

Part Ⅰ Speaking

Task 2

Directions: *Listen to the following sentences and fill in the blanks by using the words you hear. The words or phrases in Task 1 are for your reference.*

1. His knowledge and abilities to control the risks will be useful for us to move forward.
2. We would like to show our warm welcome to our guests.
3. I'd like to take a few moments to introduce our new manager.
4. Tom has worked for over 20 years in finance department, so he has got lots of financial experience.
5. Effective management essential to the development of each company.

Task 3

Directions: *Listen to the following passage and use the sentence patterns given in Task 2 to fill in the blanks.*

Dear colleagues,

   I'd like to take a few moments to introduce Jim, our new financial manager. He's new to the company and to the area, so I'm sure we'll be able to show him a warm welcome. Jim has worked for over 20 years in finance department and I know his experience will benefit us all. His knowledge of listed companies and his abilities to control the risks will be essential for us to move forward as a business.

Key to Unit 6

Part Ⅰ   Speaking

Section A

Task 1

1～5 g h c a d   6～10 b h i j e

Task 2

1. founded   2. standard   3. seat belt   4. automobile   5. performance

Task 3

1. The automobile industry in China has been flourishing in recent years.

2. Mazda company was founded in 1920.

3. The automobile of this brand is famous for its high of safety.

4. Most customers tend to have an appeal for the demand of performance in purchasing.

5. buckle your seat belt before you start to drive.

Task 4

(omitted)

Section B

Task 1

Brand Name: Mercedes-Benz   Headquartered in: Stuttgart
Product lines: Automobiles, buses, coaches and trucks

Features:		
1. high standard of quality		2. excellent performance
3. technological features		4. Incomparable comfort
Series	&	Potential Clients
Class A		familiy use
Class E		government use
Class S		symbol of the luxury cars

Task 2

(omitted)

Part Ⅱ Writing

Task 2

Beginning: <u>Paragraph one</u>
Body: <u>Paragraph two</u>
Ending: <u>Paragraph three</u>

Task 3

Situation 2

The Purchasing Behavior from Potential Customers

　　I am glad to have the opportunity to introduce to you the purchasing behavior from potential customers in the survey. Recently, with the fantastic development of science and technology, and along with the dramatic improvement in people's living standards, families have been easily affordable for two or more private cars. They will take several factors into consideration.

　　From the chart, we can see the main reasons for consumers to make a purchase of private cars is the need for excellent after-sale service, which accounts for 96.5%. Followed by performance at work (92.7%), it assures the clients of high standard quality both in driving and taking a ride. Undoubtedly, it is thought-provoking for some consumers to think of comfort as the inseparable issue, which takes up 88.4%. What are listed backward are introduction by friends (39.8%), advertising campaign (45.3%) and inner decoration (66.8%).

　　Frankly speaking, we can never imagine what our life will without private cars. The private cars do bring us more convenience than ever before. On one hand, with the increasing standard of living, people choose to enjoy sufficient interaction and timely feedback from suppliers. On the other hand, for sake of extraordinary comfort and superb after-sales service, people choose to take private cars for a journey nearby for fun.

　　To conclude, the spread of private cars, resulting from the dramatic development of economy and the pursuit of improved lifestyle, brought both convenience and rejoice. We will make the most of them. Private cars are becoming indispensable in our lives. Just have a try!

Script for Listening Comprehension

Part Ⅰ   Speaking

Task 2

Directions: *Listen to the following sentences and fill in the blanks by using the words you hear. The words or phrases in Task 1 are for your reference.*

1. Mazda Company was founded in 1920.
2. The automobile of this brand is famous for its high standard of safety.
3. Buckle your seat belt before you start to drive.
4. The automobile industry in China has been flourishing in recent years.
5. Most customers tend to have an appeal for the demand of performance in purchasing.

Task 3

Direction: *Listen to the following passage and use the sentence patterns given in Task 2 to fill in the blanks.*

　　Nowadays, automobiles play a key role in work and daily life for everyone. There are a variety of brands of cars to choose from. The automobile industry in China has been flourishing in recent years. As a creation of modern civilization, they not only provide convenience, but also have a great contribution to economic growth. For example, Mazda is a popular brand for us. Mazda Company was founded in 1920. When choosing or purchasing, customers will take several factors into consideration, such as the price, the quality of comfort, after-sale service and the performance at work. The automobile of this brand is famous for its high safety. Undoubtedly, people have different preference. Most customers tend to have an appeal for the demand of performance in purchasing. More importantly, please buckle your seat belt before you start to drive.

Part Ⅱ Writing

Task 1

Directions: *Listen to the following useful sentences which can be used to describe the pictures and charts.*

1. Our products are in superb quality, as well as the performance at work.
2. The material has a durable and easy-to-clean surface.
3. The machine will pay back your investment in 6 months.
4. The model of ... is efficient and endurable, economical and practical for middle-class people.
5. The maximum speed of this kind of automobiles is ... K/H.

Key to Test 1

Part Ⅰ Listening Comprehension

Section A（每题 1 分）

1～7. DBCDABC

Section B（每题 1 分）

8～14. CAADADB

Section C（每题 1 分）

Conversation 1

15. B   16. C

Conversation 2

17. B   18. D   19. A

Section D（每题 1 分；部分答对 0.5 分；拼写错误不给分）

20. sales manager   21. new idea   22. development   23. success   24. American market

Part Ⅱ Vocabulary & Structure

Section A（每题 1 分）

25～29. ADDCB

30～34. BBDCB

参考答案及听力原文

Section B（每题 1 分）

35. to guess　36. be made　37. frequently　38. agreement　39. more difficult

Part Ⅲ　Reading Comprehension（40—44 各 2 分，45—60 各 1 分，共 35 分）

Task 1（每题 2 分）

40～44. BCBAD

Task 2（每题 2 分）

45～47. CBD

Task 3（每题 1 分；答案超过三个词不给分）

48. 64,500　49. 2.6 million　50. the United States　51. global　52. reliable energy

Task 4（每题 1 分）

A — Luggage reclaim 认领行李　　　　B — office clerk 办公室文员

C — information desk 问询处　　　　　D — consulting director 咨询总监

E — underpass 地下通道　　　　　　　F — call for assistance 打电话咨询

G — security check 安全检查　　　　　H — waiting room 候车（机）室

I — excess baggage charge（行李超重费）　J — boarding time 登机时间

K — Don't Spit on The Floor 请勿随地吐痰　L — Cameras Forbidden 禁止拍照

M — Business As Usual 照常营业　　　　N — No Admittance 闲人免进

53. J A　54. E B　55. F H　56. K C　57. N M

Task 5（每题 1 分；答案超过三个词不给分）

58. Jim Johnson　59. General Manager　60. introduce　61. next week

62. the second floor

Part Ⅳ　Translation—English into Chinese（每题按 3 等评分：2 分，1 分，0 分）

	2 分	1 分	0 分
63	B	C	A
64	C	A	B
65	B	A	C
66	A	B	C

67.(共 7 分)

【译文】我们非常抱歉无法接受您 14 日午餐的盛情邀请。遗憾的是,我们的计划已经改变,星期一我们必须返回香港。我真心地希望在不久的将来我们还会有这样的机会,杰尼和我向你致以亲切的问候。

Part Ⅴ   Writing(共 15 分)

One possible version:

　　The conference room is available to all, but we need your help to follow the rules listed below:

1. Please keep the conference room tidy.

2. After the meeting, please take away your papers, articles and all of your personal belongings. All the electric equipment, such as, the electric lights and the air conditioner, should be shut down. All the doors and windows should be closed.

3. No smoking. No litter, please.

　　We greatly appreciate your support.

The Office
June 20th, 2017

听力原文

Part I   Listening Comprehension

Section A

1. How is everything going, Peter?

2. May I have your name please?

3. Do you like to chat in English online?

4. Would you please sign your name here, sir?

5. Do you often travel on business?

6. Can you put me through to the manager's office?

7. Shall we arrange a meeting sometime next week?

参考答案及听力原文

Section B

8. W: Tom. Why were you late for the interview?

   M: I missed the bus.

   Q: Why was Tom late?

9. W: How do you like to pay for the computer?

   W: By credit card.

   Q: How will the man pay for the computer?

10. W: We're really impressed by your work experience.

    M: Thank you very much.

    Q: What impressed the woman deeply?

11. M: Mary, why isn't Linda working here now?

    W: She retired last week.

    Q: What can we learn about Linda from the conversation?

12. M: Excuse me. Where can I learn more about your company?

    W: From our website.

    Q: Where can the man get more information about the company?

13. M: Good morning. I have an appointment with Dr. Green at 10:30.

    W: Please wait a moment. He's with another patient.

    Q: Where does the conversation most probably take place?

14. M: I'm afraid we can't have the meeting today as John isn't here.

    W: I see. Let's have it tomorrow.

    Q: When will they have the meeting?

Section C

Conversation 1

W: Good morning. May I help you?

M: Yes. I would like to see a doctor please.

W: Are you a new patient here?

M: Yes. This is my first time here.

W: I see. What's your trouble?

M: I caught a bad cold.

Q 15: What does the man want to do?

111

Q 16: What's the matter with the man?

Conversation 2

W: Good afternoon. Park Industry.

M: Hello. May I speak to Mr. Black?

W: I'm sorry. He's not in. Can I take a message?

M: Yes. I'm John Brown. Please tell him our meeting will be held on Friday at 3:30.

W: Friday at 3:30.

M: And would you tell him to call me this afternoon?

W: Yes. What's your phone number?

M: 3584058.

W: Ok. I'll pass the message to Mr. Black.

Q 17: Whom does the man want to speak to?

Q 18: When will they have the meeting?

Q 19: What will the woman do for the man?

Section D

Good afternoon, ladies and gentlemen. Thank you very much for coming to our conference this afternoon. I'm Henry Johnson, the (20) <u>sales manager</u> of Smart Toys. Now, I'd like to introduce you to a completely (21) <u>new idea</u> of toy manufacture. Firstly, I'll talk about the market research which led to the (22) <u>development</u> of this product. Then I'll explain the production and our sales plan. Finally, I'll make some suggestions so that you can make this product a (23) <u>success</u>. We are confident this new product will sell well in the (24) <u>American market</u>. At the end of my speech, we'll have a question-and-answer session.

Key to Test 2

Part Ⅰ Listening Comprehension

Section A(每题1分)

1~7. ABCADAB

参考答案及听力原文

Section B（每题 1 分）

8～14. BDACBAB

Section C（每题 1 分）

Conversation 1

15. C 16. B

Conversation 2

17. B 18. D 19. A

Section D（每题 1 分；部分答对 0.5 分；拼写错误不给分）

20. medical 21. protect 22. lower 23. lead to 24. popular

Part Ⅱ Vocabulary & Structure

Section A（每题 1 分）

25～29. CCABA

30～34. AADCB

Section B（每题 1 分）

35. wandering 36. respective 37. has been serving 38. would have finished

39. concerned

Part Ⅲ Reading Comprehension（40－44 各 2 分，45－60 各 1 分，共 35 分）

Task 1（每题 2 分）

40～44. CBCAC

Task 2（每题 2 分）

45. A 46. C 47. A

Task 3（每题 1 分；答案超过三个词不给分）

48. cheated 49. a week 50. arrival 51. cost 52. take action

Task 4（每题 1 分）

53. C Q 54. N O 55. K M 56. D L 57. P G

Task 5（每题 1 分；答案超过三个词不给分）

58. the advertisement 59. Chief office secretary 60. manufacturing company

61. foreign language 62. resume

Part Ⅳ　Translation-English into Chinese（每题按 3 等评分：2 分，1 分，0 分）

	2 分	1 分	0 分
63	B	C	A
64	C	A	B
65	A	B	C
66	B	C	A

67.（共 7 分）

【译文】如果一名人类学家想了解英国是什么样的，他可以带上他的记录本到乐购超市看看。一部分原因在于，这个超市销售英国差不多三分之一的各种物品。另一部分原因也在于，乐购超市的顾客是由富有阶层、中产阶级和贫民组成，这样的消费者比例和整个英国是完全一致的。乐购超市也像英国一样，越来越壮大。

Part Ⅴ　Writing（共 15 分）

Dear Sir or Madam,

　　I am writing to express dissatisfaction regarding accommodation. I would prefer to move into a single room next semester, as I find the present sharing arrangment inconvenient.

　　I must explain that the reason for my dissatisfaction is my roonmate's inconsiderate behavior. For one thing, his friends are constantly visiting him, for another, he regularly hold noisy parties.

　　To solve this problem, I hope to draw the attention of the authorities concerned. I am sure you will agree that the only solution for me is to move into a room of my own. Therefore, I would be grateful if you could find a single room for me, preferably not in the same building but as near to the college campus as possible.

　　　　　　　　Yours sincerely,
　　　　　　　　Mike Young

听力原文

Part I Listening Comprehension

Section A

1. Can I speak to Susan?

2. I'm terribly sorry we're late.

3. Thank you very much for your help.

4. Shall we meet again to discuss it further?

5. How does the new product sell in the market?

6. When can you leave?

7. Have you ever been to Beijing?

Section B

8. M: I wonder if you have a special menu for children.

    W: I'm sorry. But we don't have one.

    Q: What kind of food does the man ask for?

9. W: What can I do for you?

    M: I'd like to open a saving's account here.

    Q: Where does the conversation most likely take place?

10. M: Someone is knocking at the door.

    W: I think it's Jack again.

    Q: What can we learn from the conversation?

11. M: Why are you in such a hurry?

    W: I lost an important paper in the office.

    Q: Why is the woman going back to the office?

12. M: What's wrong with you, Helen?

    W: Nothing wrong. I just come from a medical check-up.

    Q: What does the woman want to do in the hospital?

13. W: May I have a look at the black jacket, please?

    M: Yes, what size do you take?

    Q: Where does this conversation most probably take place?

14. M: Will Dr. White's lecture begin at one forty or two o'clock?

    W: It will begin at one fifty and finish in two hours.

    Q: When will the lecture begin?

Section C

Conversation 1

M: Are you going to graduate this term?

W: Yes.

M: What are you going to do for a living then?

W: I'm going to be a secretary.

M: What are you supposed to do?

W: I'll work in all office, writing letters and reports, and doing some typing.

M: It must be quite boring. If I were you, I'd like to be a vet.

W: What? What does a vet do?

M: A vet is a person who takes care of sick animals. In fact, a vet is an animal doctor.

W: Animal doctor? How interesting! But how did you get the idea?

M: I once read a story about a person who treated sick animals. I'd like to have a try myself.

W: Wow, sounds exciting.

Questions:

15. What is the woman going to do when she leaves school?

16. What would the man do if he were to find a job?

Conversation 2

M: Hey, Alice. What are you doing there?

W: Hey, Roger. Could you have a look at my computer? I can't get it working.

W: Sure. Let me have a look. Hmm... It seems that the disc is jammed.

W: Oh, really? I just bought it yesterday. Well, then could you please go to the store with me? I want to have this computer replaced.

M: No problem. But you have to bring your receipt. Otherwise you can't have the computer replaced.

W: Oh, dear! I can't find my receipt. Perhaps I lost it on my way back from the store.

M: That's too bad. I'm afraid you have to find it.

W: Well, I will give you a telephone call if I can find it.

M: OK. See you then.

W: Thank you. See you.

Q 17: What's the woman's problem?

Q 18: What does the woman ask the man to do?

Q 19: What does the woman have to do to get her computer replaced?

Section D

Scientists have discovered that tea is good for us. It tastes good and it is refreshing. In recent (20) <u>medical</u> studies, tea has been found to help prevent heart attacks and cancer.

One study suggests that both black tea and green tea help (21) <u>protect</u> the heart. In the study, tea drinkers had a 44 percent (22) <u>lower</u> death rate after heart attacks than non-drinkers. Other studies have shown that tea, like fruit and vegetables, helps fight against chemicals that may (23) <u>lead to</u> the development of certain cancers.

Many people really like tea. Next to plain water, it's the world's most (24) <u>polular</u> drink.

Key to Test 3

Part Ⅰ Listening comprehension(每题1分,共24分)

Section A

1~7. ACDBCAD

Section B

8~14. ACBDCAB

Section C

15~19. CDABD

Section D(每题1分;部分答对0.5分;拼写错误不给分)

20. express   21. be proud of   22. depend on   23. ideas   24. once again

Part Ⅱ Vocabulary & Structure(每题1分,共15分)

Section A(每题1分)

25~29. BCABB

30~34. AACDB

Section B(每题1分)

35. was established   36. impression   37. to assist   38. more effective

39. meeting

Part Ⅲ Reading Comprehension (40—44各2分,45—60各1分,共35分)

Task 1(每题2分)

40~44. BADDB

Task 2(每题2分)

45. B   46. C   47. C

Task 3(每题1分;答案超过三个词不给分)

48. Committee Members   49. March 7—17   50. Omni Houston   51. US＄139

52. IEEE Transformers

Task 4(每题1分)

53. E F   54. D G   55. A I   56. B J   57. C H

Task 5(每题1分;答案超过三个词不给分)

58. today's advertisement   59. Chief Office Secretary   60. manufacturing company

61. foreign language   62. resume

Part Ⅳ Translation-English into Chinese

(63—66的评分有3个等级,分值分别是2—1—0;67题的分值为7分。总分15分。)

63. B—C—A   64. A—C—B   65. C—A—B   66. C—B—A

67. 公司取名为"苹果"是因为当时乔布斯刚从一家苹果农场回来,乔布斯当时饮食以水果为主。他认为这个名字有趣、有激情、没有攻击性。苹果公司位列《财富》杂志2008年度美国最受推崇的公司和2008年至2012年世界最受推崇的公司。

Part V Writing(共 15 分)

Overtime Request Form

Request Date：(68) March 1, 2017

Employee's Name：(69) Li Jianxin

Department：(70) Human Resources Department

Date of Overtime：March 5, 2017

Overtime needed：from (71) 9:00 a.m to 5:00 p.m.

Total Overtime：not to exceed (72) 8 hours

Reasons for Overtime Required：

Our company recently needs to recruit all kinds of employees. Human Resources Department advertised a week ago and has received many application letters. In order to assist departments to arrange the interviews, I need to work overtime on Saturday. In this way, I'll be able to get more informed about the the applicants and make a better arrangement.

听力原文

Part I Listening Comprehension

Section A

1. Can I speak to your department manager?
2. Do you know Mr. Green, the chief engineer?
3. How can I start the machine?
4. Do you enjoy traveling on business?
5. How long have you been in the new position?
6. Where do you get the information?
7. What do you think of your boss?

Section B

8. W: Do you know what day is April 22nd?

   M: It's Earth Day.

   Q: What day is April 22nd?

9. W: Do you have telephone banking service?

   W: Yes, of course.

   Q: What is the woman asking about?

10. W: Where should I sign my name?

    M: At the bottom of the page.

    Q: What does the woman want to know?

11. M: Where can I learn more about your training program?

    W: From our website.

    Q: How can the man get more information?

12. W: How does our new product sell in the market?

    M: It sells well.

    Q: What are the two speakers talking about?

13. M: When can we get our orders?

    W: You will receive them within 3 days.

    Q: What is the man asking about?

14. W: When did you start your company?

    M: In 1998. Now it has over 350 employees.

    Q: What do we know about the company from the conversation?

Section C

Conversation 1

W: You seem quite busy these days.

M: Yes. We're doing a market survey.

W: Really? What is it about?

M: About people's attitude toward online shopping.

W: What results have you got?

M: Most young people prefer shopping online.

W: How about old people?

M: Some old people also like online shopping.

Q15: What is the man doing these days?

Q16: What can we learn about online shopping from the conversation?

Conversation 2

M: Hi, Jenny. I've found a summer job.

W: That's fine.

M: I'll be working at Disney Land!

W: Wow! Sounds great!

M: How about you, Jenny?

W: I've got an offer, as a tour guide.

M: But a tour guide has to work long hours.

W: That is why I haven't made up my mind yet.

Q17: What do we learn about the man?

Q18: What job is offered to the woman?

Q19: Why hasn't the woman made up her mind to accept the job?

Section D

Good evening, ladies and gentlemen!

First of all, I'd like to (20) express a sincere welcome to you all, the new comers of our company. As you know, our company is one of the top 50 companies in the country and has a history of more than 100 years. I think you must (21) be proud of being a member of such a great company. But we cannot (22) depend on tradition alone. We need new employees with new knowledge and creative (23) ideas.

I would like to welcome you (24) once again, and from today, let's begin to work together.

Key to Test 4

Part I Listening Comprehension

Section A（每题1分）
1~7. ADDBBAA

Section B（每题 1 分）

8～14. AABAADB

Section C（每题 1 分）

Conversation 1

15. B 16. D

Conversation 2

17. C 18. A 19. B

Section D（每题 1 分；部分答对 0.5 分；拼写错误不给分）

20. critical 21. consumer 22. horsepower 23. fuel 24. culturally

Part Ⅱ Vocabulary & Structure

Section A（每题 1 分）

25～29. BBCBC

30～34. ACDCC

Section B（每题 1 分）

35. had finished 36. have seen 37. is 38. are 39. the earlier/sooner

Part Ⅲ Reading Comprehension（40—44 各 2 分，45—60 各 1 分，共 35 分）

Task 1（每题 2 分）

40～44. BBBBD

Task 2（每题 2 分）

45. C 46. B 47. D

Task 3（每题 1 分；答案超过三个词不给分）

48. accurate learning experience 49. working 50. suitable 51. excellent managers

52. confident

Task 4（每题 1 分）

53. I A 54. F C 55. D J 56. E B 57. L K

Task 5（每题 1 分；答案超过三个词不给分）

58. data recovery 59. Britain 60. lost his data 61. 30 years

62. experienced engineers

Part Ⅳ　Translation-English into Chinese（每题按 3 等评分：2 分，1 分，0 分）

	2 分	1 分	0 分
63	A	B	C
64	A	B	C
65	C	A	B
66	A	C	B

67.（共 7 分）

【译文】如今的汽车都已安装了一种转换器。当废气排入这种转换器"盒子"中时，其内部的一种化学制剂会把废气中的有害物质分解成害处较小的化学物质。但是，仍然有些污染物质会流入大气中形成烟雾，这种烟雾会烧灼你的眼睛、鼻子和喉咙，而且使你呼吸困难。

Part Ⅴ　Writing（共 15 分）

(1) Li Menghua

(2) Female

(3) August 19th, 1995

(4) 18654789652

(5) Sep. 2012—July 2016　Majored in Automobile Marketing and Planning in Donghai University；

　　2013　Got a driver's license；2015－2016　Won the annual scholarship twice；

　　2016　Passed CET-6 and National Computer Examination Level Ⅱ

(6) Sep. 2015—now　Internship in BMW 4S store

听力原文

Part Ⅰ　Listening Comprehension

Section A

1. May I know your address?

2. It's so nice to meet you here, Sam. I am so happy.

3. What does your sister look like?

4. How often do you do yoga?

5. Excuse me, have you got a map of America?

6. How much is the ticket to Malaysia, please?

7. May I speak to Mr. Gump?

Section B

8. W: Mr. Johnson will be back in a few minutes. You can wait if you want to.

   M: No, thanks. I'll just leave this message for him.

   Q: What does the man ask the woman to do?

9. W: I want to mail this box to London.

   W: By ordinary or express?

   Q: Where is the man?

10. W: Was it hot here last summer?

    M: Yes, it was. August was much hotter than July and September.

    Q: Which month was the hottest one last summer?

11. M: What do you think of the food here?

    W: Delicious. I think we'll come again this weekend.

    Q: Where does the conversation take place?

12. M: Thomas, how do you come to our company, by bus or by bike?

    W: Well, I take the underground.

    Q: How does Thomas come to his company?

13. M: Is it raining outside?

    W: Yes, very heavily. We have to cancel the football game.

    Q: What's the speaker's plan?

14. M: Haven't you finished the book yet?

    W: Almost. I've only one-fifth of the pages left.

    Q: How many pages has the woman read?

Section C

Conversation 1

Instructor: Ok, so you are sitting in the car. What do you do now?

参考答案及听力原文

Learner: Well, I'll first start the car. No, wait! I check behind me first before I drive away.

Instructor: You've forgotten something.

Learner: Oh, yes. I need to fasten my seat belt first.

Q 15: What does the man want to do at first?

Q 16: What should the man do at first?

Conversation 2

M: Good morning. Honda Automobile.

W: Hello. May I speak to Mr. Simpson?

M: I'm sorry. He's not in. Can I take a message?

W: Yes. This is Ellen Parker. Please tell him our appointment has to be put off till next Friday afternoon.

M: Next Friday afternoon.

W: And would you please tell him to call me back this afternoon?

M: Sure. What's your phone number?

W: 68745219.

M: Ok. I'll pass the message to Mr. Simpson.

Q 17: Whom does the woman want to speak to?

Q 18: When will they have the meeting?

Q 19: What's the woman's phone number?

Section D

While automobiles are a (20) critical part of any transportation system, car culture makes it difficult to create sustainable urban transport. When (21) consumer demand calls for size and (22) horsepower—not mobility or sustainability—(23) fuel efficiency is quickly sacrificed. Moreover, when cars become so (24) culturally valued rather than simply functionally important, necessary reforms for sustainable transport become difficult.